THE SACRED
HERBS OF
SAMHAIN

"*The Sacred Herbs of Samhain* offers even more than bringing us into the magical world of spirits and fairies! I recommend that anyone fascinated by herbs embark on a literary herbal foray with Ellen Evert Hopman. Her in-depth knowledge of herbs provides a unique reference resource for the harvesting techniques, preparation methods, dosages, cautions, and use details for both physical and spiritual healing, complete with the fragrance of informative ancestral herbal lore."

KATHY-ANN BECKER, AUTHOR OF *SILENCING THE WOMEN: THE WITCH TRIALS OF MARY BLISS PARSONS*

"Based on her impressive knowledge of herbs and the old-time practices of wise and witchy forest wives, Hopman offers a compendium of herbal medicinals in *The Sacred Herbs of Samhain*. A compelling look into Celtic herbal practices connected to the autumnal time of year when days are short and the veil between life and death is thin. The contents include all the how-tos and why you'd want-tos and why nots, with clear identification for practical and ritual usage provided by image and description. Beyond the practical are the entertaining, engaging tales of folk and fairy, of goddess and god, and of prophetic romance and/or death. This book is an invitation to delve into the shadows and realms of time gone by, the origins of the hallowed days of Samhain, Halloween, and other worldwide observances. A guide to keep by your side."

MARYLYN MOTHERBEAR SCOTT, POET, AUTHOR, AND FOUNDER AND HIGH PRIESTESS OF MAGICKAL CAULDRON

"A delightful collection of herbal knowledge and Celtic lore for Samhain. In addition to providing a significant reference on relevant magical and medicinal uses for herbs, trees, and more, Ellen provides complete instructions for a Samhain ritual and also a traditional Dumb Supper. Her easy-to-follow recipes for soup, breads, soul cake, dumb cake, magical ink, and even dandelion wine complete this gem. Recommended."

MORVEN WESTFIELD, AUTHOR OF *THE OLD POWER RETURNS*

"Another jewel in Ellen Evert Hopman's collection, *The Herbs of Samhain* sparkles from beginning to end—from how to stay alive and dig mandrake to making elderberry sorbet and crowns of mallow leaves to how to spot where the fairies did battle the night before. I was entertained, challenged, and enthralled with each turn of the page as I partook of eclectic knowledge, Druid teachings, poetry, and recipes that have inspired me to more deeply weave herbs into my Samhain tradition. No doubt I'll be coming back to this book many, many times!"

WENDY SNOW FOGG, FOUNDER AND SENIOR HERBALIST OF
MISTY MEADOWS HERBAL CENTER IN LEE, NEW HAMPSHIRE

"Ellen Evert Hopman provides a potent reminder that it's the relationship between the living and the dead that lies at the very heart of Samhain and Halloween. This crucial point is all too often overlooked amid all the commercialization and sensationalism that in recent years has come to surround this most profound of holidays. This book is a practical, comprehensive, clear, and useful guide to a wide variety of plants together with a great selection of spells, recipes, and fairy lore."

JUDIKA ILLES, AUTHOR OF *ENCYCLOPEDIA OF 5000 SPELLS*

"Ellen Hopman's book is a treasure trove of herbal knowledge and wisdom. A great read!"

RICK ALLEN, GRAMMY NOMINEE AND AUTHOR OF
F 'N' A!: MY CRAZY LIFE IN ROCK AND BLUES

THE SACRED
HERBS OF
SAMHAIN

Plants
to Contact
the Spirits of
the Dead

ELLEN EVERT HOPMAN

DESTINY

BOOKS

Destiny Books
Rochester, Vermont

Destiny Books
One Park Street
Rochester, Vermont 05767
www.DestinyBooks.com

Destiny Books is a division of Inner Traditions International

Note to the reader: This book is intended as an informational guide. The remedies, approaches, and techniques described herein are meant to supplement, and not to be a substitute for, professional medical care or treatment. They should not be used to treat a serious ailment without prior consultation with a qualified health care professional.

Cataloging-in-Publication Data for this title is available from the Library of Congress

ISBN 978-1-62055-861-4 (print)
ISBN 978-1-62055-862-1 (ebook)

Printed and bound in the United States

10 9 8 7 6 5 4 3 2

Text design and layout by Virginia Scott Bowman

This book was typeset in Garamond Premier Pro with Thirsk and Albertus used as display typefaces

To send correspondence to the author of this book, mail a first-class letter to the author c/o Inner Traditions • Bear & Company, One Park Street, Rochester, VT 05767, and we will forward the communication, or contact the author directly at **www.elleneverthopman.com.**

CONTENTS

ℱOREWORD
By Andrew Theitic

The spirit of Samhain casts a deep, mysterious shadow through all facets of our world. Those of a mystical nature will naturally sense the shroud between the worlds thinning as the summer days of heat and lush flora begin to subside, replaced with autumn's chill breezes and flame-colored leaves. With the approach of the Hallows season, even the most mundane of our acquaintances will also begin to ramble on about strange sounds in the night, deceased relatives visiting them in dreams, shadows staring at them or acting strangely. It cannot be helped.

It's no wonder that society should feel this way. The gradual decline of the sun's arc, the shortening of daylight and lengthening of the nocturnal, the first raw winds and wild storms that batter our homes and lives, and the eventual rebirth and renewal of bud have been immortalized in legends, fables, and folklore throughout the world. In our common mythology, goblins and ghosts, both literal and figurative, return each year to haunt the land. It was not merely the changing temperature or solar fluctuations that nabbed human attentions, but the seemingly sudden loss of the Earth's prosperity in such a beautifully dramatic fashion.

In the Northern Hemisphere—particularly in those areas with latitudes close to the pole—there are few seasonal shifts more striking than the splendidly colorful change from summer's heat to winter's frost, accompanied by the perceptual withering and demise of the local flora before their inevitable rebirth. It is ironically these transitional times that tend to bring us back to ourselves, connecting us to the abode between the world of matter and spirit, and invoking the inevitable spiritual "regroupings" that occur at these times.

In the mundane world, we begin to gather together in celebration of the harvest's bounty, enjoying newly stoked fires, hot drinks, and seasonal delicacies with our family, friends, and neighbors. But those gatherings are not only mundane. Throughout the centuries, our families, clans, and villages—as well as groups of like-minded spiritual seekers— also brought to the hearths and bonfires those herbs deemed sacred to gods, magic, and the ancient mystical traditions.

Most obviously, the death of warmth and abundance points to the inevitable death of us all one day, and the massive debt each of us owes to the land, the harvest, and the lines of our ancestors stretching back to the dawn of time. Along similar lines, it is best to acknowledge that we owe our very earthly existence to the constant influence of the botanical world. From the food we eat to the air we breathe, we are forever indebted to our bountiful allies for the gift of life.

Working with plants is a most rewarding hobby, as we learn to tend and befriend these sometimes alien-seeming life-forms. Not surprisingly, those of a mystical bent in ancient times found each plant to have a particular spirit connected to it, as well as affinities with specific animals and fairies among the Greenwood.

Throughout history, many of our most ancient texts and writings have been lost, yet our link to the flora of our world has remained ever constant. At first, photosynthetic respiration may seem the most important part of our relationship with plants. Then again, handed down through generations of interaction with these beautifully complex organisms have been fables and myths, rhymes, charms, and brilliant bits of folklore woven through with the joys and sorrows of our lives, manifesting the manner in which we are bound to the land for our very survival. Only now, in our modern era of city streets and easily delivered conveniences, do we feel divorced from the Earth and the countless species of trees, plants, lichen, and fungi that surround us. However, the plants remain forever living, thriving, and awaiting our attention. They come to us as foods and flavorings, as medicine, as spiritual and magical foci, as incense for strewing and scenting the home, or as gateways toward mind-altering experiences—or all of the above.

As the seasons reflect the thinning of the shroud or veil—the theoretical psychic membrane between the worlds of flesh and spirit—so do those of an occult persuasion look to Mother Nature for a means of contact between these worlds. Rite, ritual, and herbal extraction combine with spiritual focus as the adept first turns inward in reflection before leaping outward in astral projection. Meditation, the use of potent botanicals, and ecstatic trance and dance have been used for thousands of years, and still are, to forge new pathways of consciousness and perception, deepening the seeker's wisdom with the aid of spiritual and chemical allies found nearly everywhere the adept is willing to look.

This path, like most, is strewn with traps and pitfalls. Many a courageous explorer, herbalist, and Witch has paid a steep, if not final, price for meddling disrespectfully with the more dangerous plants of the pharmacopeia, be they psychotropic, deliria-inducing, or downright venomous. Even seemingly innocuous herbs can contain toxins and alkaloids that can cause discomfort and pain in the hardiest of individuals. Conveniently, our ancestors had much to say concerning these plants. Evidence about their reactions and relations to seasons, animals, and we humans fortunately was preserved for the contemporary Witch and magician alike. In addition, they also had much to say about the myriad spirits tied to the plants, the forest glades and underworld gateways, odd stones and ancient burial mounds, the portals between this world and those glimpsed only by folks daring enough to search for them.

So, with decades of experience in both the mystical and mundane expressions of the Greenwood's prosperity, you will be hard-pressed to find a more experienced and friendly guide through Samhain's haunted, leaf-strewn woods than Ellen Evert Hopman, who knows the hooks and crooks of the road as well as its best picnic areas. When wandering paths lined with dangerous denizens, like the screaming Mandrake, the stunning Aconitum or Wolfsbane, and the dread lady *Atropa belladonna,* these are necessary attributes indeed. With a keen eye and a Druid's touch, she'll steer you clear of accidental poisoning and hospital trips while keeping the practical in mind, the ingredients fresh, and the recipes easy to follow, all the while allowing the mystical lore its fair share of breath and expression. Let's take a walk, shall we?

ANDREW THEITIC lives in Providence, Rhode Island, with his husband and two magnificent dogs. He is the publisher and editor of *The Witches' Almanac* and has been a practicing Witch and magician since the early 1970s. In addition, he chairs several nonprofit organizations that benefit the Craft, magical, and Pagan communities.

ᴀᴄᴋɴᴏᴡʟᴇᴅɢᴍᴇɴᴛꜱ

I wish to thank Kevin Sartoris of Muse Gifts & Books in Marlborough, New Hampshire, who invited me to speak at the annual "Celebrate Samhain" event and suggested that I talk about herbs to contact the dead. I said, "Sure," and promptly put together a talk. Then Kevin asked, "Why not make the talk into a book?" and I said, "Why not?" and this volume was born. Thanks are also due to Michael J. Masley for assistance with Egyptian herb magic. Many thanks to Ari Kinehan for invaluable recipes and suggestions and to David Salisbury for further details about flying ointments. Thank you to Gwennic for approving the Mórrigan rite (he assures me that the Mórrigan approves also). Thanks to Morven Westfield for astute comments and suggestions.

An Introduction to Samhain, the Otherworld, and the Power of Herbs

It is the eve of Samhain, and I am fortunate to have been invited to a Witches' observance, just down the street from my rural home. The altar is set up outside, resplendent with produce from the garden, candles, and pictures of ancestors who have crossed the veil. Dishes of food are placed nearby for the enjoyment of the dead. Even the cats get their due—a plate of tuna has been set out, just for all our deceased feline familiars.

The altar is covered with dead, dried plants. If you look closely, each dried plant is bearing seeds, the promise of new life amid death. Everyone is urged to reflect on that truth: that every death we experience is but an opening to the next realm of existence. The seeds remind us to hold on to a dream all through the dark of winter, knowing that the dream will slowly come into being as the warmth of spring returns.

Next, we call upon our own beloved dead, those who laughed and cried and toiled and sacrificed just so that we could be here enjoying life today. We tell their stories and give them thanks.

We feel fortunate to have come through yet another year, for who knows if and when our own crossing of the veil will occur. We end by sharing food and drink. Feasting together by the warm fire, we assure

1

ourselves and each other that we will survive the coming dark and cold of winter.

Samhain is a great fire festival of the ancient Celts, celebrated at the official close of the harvest. By Samhain all the produce of the fields must be safely gathered into the house and barn, and anything left in the fields after this date is the property of the *sidhe* (pronounced "she" and meaning the fairies, sometimes known as the Good Neighbors) and not to be touched by mortals. It is an old Celtic tradition to leave offerings for the fairies on this potent spirit night.

Samhain marks the end of the Celtic year and, after a three-day observance, the beginning of the next agricultural cycle. Just as a seed begins its existence in the dark of the soil, so does the new year begin in the dark of winter, which is the time to rest, take stock of the past year's accomplishments, and dream of future goals.

For the ancient Celts there were only two seasons, summer and winter, the light half of the year and the dark half of the year. The festivals of Samhain and Beltaine (May Day) were portals between these two spheres of existence, times of chaos when the Otherworld more easily bled through. Samhain, like Beltaine, was a potent spirit night, a liminal time when the walls between the worlds were thin and ancestral spirits roamed the Earth. It was a good time for divination and contact with the Otherworld.

Following is an example from Ireland.

One activity involved setting several objects out in saucers or plates, which were then laid on a table. The chosen objects varied from one region to another, and even between different households, but generally a few of the following were included; a ring, a piece of wood, clay, a bean, a coin, salt, water, a button or a thimble. Once the saucers were set, a blindfolded person seated before them would pick one, the item which the person touched was symbolically believed to indicate their future situation in life. A ring meant the person would be married, a piece of wood or clay meant that they would die young, a bean or a rag meant that they would always be poor, while a coin indicated that they would be wealthy, salt was for luck, water meant that the person would emigrate or travel, while if one picked the saucer with a button or thimble it was believed they would die a bachelor or a spinster.[1]

Herbs can be powerful allies in any engagements with the spirit world, especially during Samhain, when the doors to the spirit world lie open. Among other things, the herbs profiled in this book can help you voyage to the Otherworld, communicate with spirits, or protect yourself against malevolent energies. As with all of my books, I have also discussed the medicinal properties of the herbs, because I feel that it rounds out the picture of each plant. Ancient herbalists, Witches, and Druid healers would have had a deep knowledge of each plant they worked with, both for magic and for medicine. **Please pay careful attention to the cautions for each herb!**

Voyaging to the Otherworld

Celtic poets had various names for the Otherworld: "Honeyed Plain of Bliss," "Apple Island," "Fortunate Island," "Summerland," and "Isles of the Blessed." Why go there? Perhaps to divine your life's purpose, to enhance your creative work, or to meet spirit guides, ancestors, Otherworldly beings, or just the invisible nature spirits dwelling on the other side of the veil.

Before journeying to meet these beings, you must be well grounded, because this is practical work, not mere glamour. You should already have a strong sense of your spiritual path and not be unduly swayed by the beings you encounter. The goal is to travel and return, changed but wiser, and ethically uncompromised.

Where is the Otherworld best found? Tradition tells us to seek for it in liminal spaces: between the land and the water, at the break of day or night, or at dusk, midnight, or dawn. Underground openings— in the recesses of a cave, or in a fairy hill or sidhe mound—are potent entrances to this world. It may also be encountered under the waves, on an island, in a dark forest, on the other side of a waterfall or mist, across a wide open plain, beyond the horizon, at the shore of a lake or pool, or on a mountain peak. Sometimes it can even be glimpsed within a fire.

Once the Otherworld is reached, the visitor finds that it is beyond space and time and free from intellectual limitation. Between the realms of chaos and the ultimate ground of all being, it splits reason to reveal the subconscious architecture of the universal mind.

The ultimate Otherworld journey begins at our own death, and at Samhain we leave out dishes of food and offerings of drink for the ancestors who have already made the trip. As the final voyage approaches, Celts will call upon Manannán Mac Lir, god of the headlands and son of the sea, possessor of the magical crane bag of power—a magical bag containing many physical treasures—to ride across the waves and carry the departed across the ocean swells to the Isles of the Blessed. The crane bag may also be a reference to the ancient Ogham alphabet of the Druids and Bards because the Ogham ciphers could have been suggested by the legs of flying cranes.

There are many ways by which you might know that someone will soon make that journey. You might see their "cowalker" (or fairy double) after the noon hour. A mouse squeaking loudly under the bed, a raven flying over the house, a cock crowing at midnight, and loud ringing in the ears are possible signs. Other death omens include a dog howling at night, shying away from a sick person, or barking three times; a crow or magpie landing on the roof, especially if an owl hoots nearby; the sound of water dripping or of strange knocking; a coffin-shaped coal leaping from the fire; the ticking of the woodworm; the song of a quail; or feathers drifting to the ground.

If you dream of a ship sailing on dry land, or if the ends of a rainbow both fall within a single township, or if, when a sailing man's pants are washed, they fill with water, a death is near.

Other signs are a bull roaring at night, the appearance of a bird in the house, a meteor, or the cry of the banshee (a fairy woman) who shrieks along the processional route a funeral will take. Someone with "the sight" might see a funeral shroud wrapped around a person. And sometimes a "death candle" is seen—a bright light that illuminates a room in the dead of night, looking like a blue or green luminous mass that rolls as if pushed by an invisible hand.

Herbal Protection in
This Realm and Others

According to Celtic tradition, the dead come to visit the living at Samhain, especially in the dark of night. A welcome is extended to these wandering dead by leaving a door open, setting an extra plate of food at the table, and placing an extra seat near the hearth. Candles are lit and placed in windows and doorways to light the way home for departed ancestors.

But it is understood that not all of these ancestors are happy and that some might come to take revenge for slights inflicted upon them in their previous life. Samhain is the time when vengeful ghosts find it easiest to cross the veil and exact retribution. Ghosts are known to seek out and follow those with whom they have a grudge, and if you hear footsteps behind you, it can be deadly to turn around and look to see who is there. If you have to be outside, it is wise to go in disguise so as not to be recognized by vengeful spirits.

But it's not only ghosts that we need to be shielded from, for who among us has not needed protection from the living from time to time? I vividly remember a Midsummer's Eve when I decided to do an all-night vigil on top of a hill. I carefully packed a large woven basket with a rattle for singing songs, some food and drink, and a spray of Oak, a tree without which no Druid will perform a ceremony, according to ancient reports. I also donned a navy-blue cape with a large hood.

I climbed the hill in the dark, leaving my car at the base. The first few hours of the vigil passed without incident. Then I heard a crowd of very drunk college-age boys laughing and joking as they wound their way closer and closer. I didn't think there would be trouble, but when one of them saw me he began to scream, "A witch!" "Get the witch!" they shouted as they moved in my direction with inebriated stumbles.

Now I was becoming scared. I pulled the hood over my face, clutched the Oak branch, and sank into the tall grass. The drunks kept circling around me screaming about "killing the witch," but they couldn't find me in the dark. Even though I was just a few feet away, I had become invisible. Finally, they gave up in disgust and careened back down the hillside, and I completed my vigil in peace.

A Primer on Herbal Preparation

Before we foray into the herbs that protect us and help us contact the spirits, let's talk about the different methods of finding and preparing herbs.

Finding Good-Quality Herbs

You can grow herbs yourself, purchase them from commercial growers, or wild-craft—that is, collect them from the wild. However, there are some considerations to take into account.

First, before you head into the wild to gather plants, make sure of their status in your area. A number of the plants listed in this book are now threatened or endangered due to overharvesting and habitat loss. Keep the following rule in mind: "Walk by the first seven, leave the eighth for the animals, and you may take the ninth." This practice ensures conservation; there will be enough plants left in the wild to produce seed for the following year, and the creatures of the wild will have the food they depend on.

Because overharvesting of wild populations is such a problem, do not purchase wild-crafted herbs unless you know they are of a species that is very abundant. Instead, purchase commercially grown herbs. Be sure that these herbs are organic, because nonorganic commercially grown herbs tend to be heavily contaminated with pesticides. This is especially true for plants that come from other countries (China, India); imported plants may also be irradiated.

How to Make a Tea

Herbal teas can generally be divided into two categories—infusions and decoctions—depending on which part of the plant is being brewed. The rule of thumb is that flowers and leaves, being more delicate plant parts, are prepared as infusions, while the tougher plant parts, like roots, barks, and seeds, are prepared as decoctions.

- **Infusion:** Bring water to a boil, pour the hot water over the herbs, cover, and let steep for about 20 minutes.
- **Decoction:** Combine the water and herbs in a nonaluminum pot, cover tightly, bring to a simmer, and let simmer for about 20 minutes. (Never boil your herbs; they will lose their volatile oils through the steam.)

Whether you're making an infusion or a decoction, the usual proportions are 2 teaspoons of herbs per cup of water (use a bit more if the herbs are fresh—about 2½ teaspoons). The dose is ¼ cup taken four times a day, not with meals. The idea is to have a small amount of the herb in your system all day.

How to Make a Salve

Put your fresh, wilted, or dry herbs in a nonaluminum pot and add just enough cold-pressed virgin oil (olive oil is the best one for general purposes) to barely cover them. Keep careful track of how much oil you pour into the pot.

Cover the pot, bring the oil to a simmer, and let simmer (do not boil) for at least 20 minutes. Or bring to a simmer and then turn off the heat, repeating that process several times a day for a week, allowing the herbs to steep continuously in the hot oil.

In a separate pot, bring beeswax to the same temperature as the simmering hot oil. Put 3 to 4 tablespoons of hot beeswax per cup of oil used into the pot with the herbs. Stir well and then strain the hot mixture into very clean glass jars or metal tins. Cap tightly and store in a cool, dark place.

How to Make a Poultice

Put fresh herbs into a blender (or pour boiling hot water over dried herbs to make them soft and then put them in the blender). Add just enough water so that you can blend the herbs into a "mush."

Pour the mush into a bowl and mix in just enough powdered slippery elm bark for the mixture to take on the consistency of pie dough. Lightly knead the mixture into a ball.

Set the ball on a clean cloth. Use a rolling pin or an old bottle to roll it out flat. Apply to the body, laying the flattened herb mixture directly on your skin and wrapping the cloth as needed to hold it in place. Keep the poultice on for 1 hour, then remove it and discard the herb mixture.

Poultices are best applied cold, so try making them ahead of time and freezing them or storing them in the refrigerator before use.

How to Make a Fomentation

A fomentation is like a hot, moist poultice. First, steam or simmer the herbs in a very minimal amount of water until soft. Soak a very clean cloth in the herbal brew and then lay out the hot cloth on a plate. Transfer the cooked herbs to the cloth and fold it to keep the herbs inside. Apply to the body while still warm.

How to Make a Tincture

Pack your herbs into a glass jar and add just enough vodka to barely cover them. (Plain vodka is best, although anything that is at least 80 percent alcohol, such as whiskey, will do in a pinch.) Cap tightly and let steep, shaking the jar periodically (at least a few times a week).

Pay careful attention to your herbs. When the plant matter begins to break down—this can take a just few hours for flowers, a few days for leaves, and a few weeks for roots, barks, berries, or fungi—strain out the liquid. Store the tincture in a dark place or in blue or brown glass bottle. Be sure to put a label on the bottle so you remember what it is!

Adding a few drops of vegetable glycerin to the "mother tincture" (I use about 1 teaspoon per quart) will make the tincture more bioavailable. Vegetable glycerin increases the valency of the herb's molecules, meaning that each molecule will have more electrons sticking out of it so that the body's receptors will have an easier time latching on.

The usual dose for tinctures is 20 drops, taken in hot tea or water, three or four times a day. That dose assumes a 150-pound person. Someone who weighs significantly more or less should adjust the dose accordingly; for example, a 75-pound person would get half the usual dose.

Some edible herbs, including Cayenne, Lobelia, Nettles, Dandelion, Violet flower, Chive blossom, and Red Clover, are best tinctured in vinegar rather than vodka. Vinegar tinctures are helpful for children and for people who wish to avoid alcohol. Vinegar tinctures last about two years, while alcohol tinctures last about five years.

Cautions

Many herbs should be avoided by people with a number of medical conditions, like diabetes or high blood pressure, and by people who are taking certain medications, whether over-the-counter or prescription. So, if you have any serious health problems or are taking any medication and you want to try using a particular herb, please check the contraindications for that herb. You can search online for "herb-drug interaction" or use the Natural Medicines Comprehensive Database (naturalmedicines .com). WebMD often has good advice too, and an herbalist or naturopath will be able to give you good guidance as well.

The same holds true if you are pregnant or breastfeeding—check for contraindications before beginning to use an herb. Some herbs can lead to complications in pregnancy, while others are unsafe for infants and can be passed through to them via the mother's breast milk.

As is the case with most foods and medicines, herbs that are perfectly safe for most people can stimulate a bad reaction in certain individuals. So, if you have never used a particular herb, before diving in, first try a small amount and see how it affects you.

Above all, if I say something is poisonous, I mean it! If an herb is especially dangerous but you'd still like to use it, you can safely partake of it via a homeopathic dilution or flower essence.

Homeopathic Dilutions

Homeopathic remedies are "energy medicines" that go directly into the vital force, or chi, of the body, bypassing digestion. Plants prepared homeopathically are tinctured in alcohol and then repeatedly diluted in alcohol, often until no molecule of the original plant is left. What remains is the energy signature of the plant.

Homeopathic medicines are usually soaked into globules of milk sugar (*Saccharum lactis*), which are easy and pleasant to swallow.

The usual homeopathic recommendation is to take the remedy (the vial will tell you how much and how often) until you feel a change and then stop. Homeopathic plant medicines are very safe if not taken too often or for too long a period, and they can be canceled out by drinking black coffee, eating mint candies, wearing heavy perfume, the smell of camphor (as in mothballs), dental work, and airplane travel.

Flower Essences

If you are fortunate enough to have access to live plants (organically grown) with flowers, another way to safely partake of a plant's unique energetic signature is to make a flower essence. The method is simple but profound. Collect the fresh flowers and place them in a crystal bowl. The bowl should be one that you reserve just for making flower essences from this particular plant, because glass is porous and it will absorb the color and signature of every plant you put into it. Just barely cover the flowers with fresh springwater and leave the bowl on the earth for 4 hours on a cloudless day, exposed to the full sun. This is not a "sun tea," however, and the water should remain clear.

If you don't have the heart to cut off living flowers, just place the crystal bowl directly under the plant and use a gentle weight to carefully bend the flowers into the water in the bowl. Make sure the bowl will be in full sun for 4 full hours on a cloudless day.

After 4 hours, carefully filter the plant material from the water. Preserve the flower essence by adding enough alcohol to make up about one-third of the total volume. Edward Bach used peach brandy. I like to use Leroux natural fruit flavor Triple Sec liqueur for the taste.

Now you have a flower essence "mother tincture." To prepare the essence for dosing, place 8 drops of this mother tincture in a sterilized (boiled for 20 minutes) 1-ounce glass dropper bottle that has been filled with springwater. The usual dose is 4 drops of the prepared essence, taken four times a day, at least 1 hour before or after a meal. In the early morning upon rising and late at night before retiring are the most important times to absorb the essence. The former sets up your daily activity and the latter sets up your dreaming.

It is best to work with just one flower essence at a time because the single signature sends a strong message to your psyche. You can combine up to three essences in one formula, but more than that becomes too confusing for your nervous system and mind to process effectively.

If you are healthy, if you are not taking medications, and if you pay careful attention to the cautions associated with each plant, you should be able to work with the herbs as described in the following chapters. Alternatively, you can simply place them on your altar or wear them on your person as a crown or in an amulet bag, charm bag, mojo bag, or medicine bundle.

PART ONE

❧

HERBS OF THE SPIRITS AND THE DEAD AND HOW TO USE THEM AT SAMHAIN

ᴴERBS FOR ᴾROTECTION FROM AND ᶜOMMUNICATION WITH THE ᔆPIRITS AND ᶠAIRIES

Any time you take steps to communicate with Otherworld entities, it is wise to first set up protection for yourself. Make sure you are well grounded as you begin, perhaps taking a few minutes to feel the Earth beneath your feet and the strength and support she gives you. Slow down and deepen your breathing, noticing your diaphragm and how it fills and empties like a sail in the wind.

When you are centered in your heart and ready for the work, open your eyes and reread the magical notes and preparation instructions for the herbs you have selected for protection. If you will be breathing in or ingesting an herb, please note the cautions associated with that plant and take them very seriously.

When you are sure that you can safely interact with the herbs you have chosen, you can call upon the gods, goddesses, and angelic entities with whom you work. Ask them to surround you with their protection and guidance. Proceed with a mature and sober attitude and all will be well!

Aconite, Monkshood, Wolfsbane
(*Aconitum napellus*)

Aconite root is an herb of the Angel of Death that is burned at funerals and planted on graves. It was once mixed with Henbane (*Hyoscyamus niger*), Belladonna (*Atropa belladonna*), Water Hemlock (*Cicuta virosa*), and soot in flying ointments. (The soot was added so that practitioners could see exactly how much they had applied.) These ointments would have been made by simmering the herbs in butter, suet, or lard. Once the ointment was applied, a practitioner could travel to the astral realms.

Aconite is probably most useful in helping practitioners contact werewolves. In fact, Wolfsbane was an ingredient in salves once used by shape-shifters to turn themselves into werewolves. In my opinion, these creatures are denizens of the astral plane and one needs to journey there to find them. (Similarly, the Sasquatch or "bigfoot" is also a creature of the astral plane and essentially a type of fairy. This is why many people see them, yet they can never be found.)

"In Europe such plants, including the nightshade datura stramonium linked to witches' flying ointment, have also been indicated in cases of shape-shifting and lycanthropy. A detailed recipe for werewolf salve provided by Jean de Nynauld in *De La Lycanthropie, Transformation, et Extase des Sorciers* (Paris, 1615), and quoted at length by Weyer, included "belladonna root, henbane, and aconite, also known as wolfsbane or monkshood."[1]

> **CAUTION: Aconite and other herbs traditionally used in these formulas are dangerous and could be fatal if ingested or if too much is spread on the skin. Also, I have never yet found an actual traditional formula that provided the exact amounts of these herbs to use, so please don't try this at home or you may be visiting the Otherworld in person sooner than you wish!**

When worn, Aconite also offers protection from werewolves and vampires, and you can carry a bit of the root in a bag (so it doesn't touch your skin) as protection when you travel alone on a dark night.

It has been said that *A. napellus* came from the splattered saliva of Cerberus, the three-headed guard dog of the gates of Hades: "There is a hidden cave that leads to a dark chasm with a steep downward path, and up this path Hercules dragged Cerberus on a steel chain, the monstrous dog resisting all the way, blinking from the light, turning his eyes away from the sun's bright rays, enraged, filling the air with barking from all three mouths at once, and spattering the green fields with drops of foamy saliva. The saliva hardened, people think, and, fed by the rich and fertile soil, became a lethal poison. And because it was formed and grows on hard stones, farmers call it 'aconite.'"[2]

Though Aconite is a deadly herb that should not be taken internally, very dilute homeopathic doses are fine. Homeopaths safely use Aconite to treat shock, fear, acute sudden fevers and flu, and conditions that come on suddenly in a cold wind.

A small amount of Aconite can be useful topically as an anesthetic—for example, in salves for joint pain and arthritis. What is a "small amount"? "The 1968 Medicines Act recommends the use of aconite in topical preparations that does not exceed 1.3 parts of aconite to 100 parts of the topical applicant. This has been found to be below the amount that may cause a toxic reaction."[3] Do not apply the salve to broken skin.

Aconite at Samhain

Make a small cloth mojo bag to hang around your neck. Place a bit of Aconite root inside. When handling the root, be sure to wear plastic gloves.

Apple Tree
(*Malus* spp.)

The Apple is a symbol of the Otherworld; cut an Apple in half and you will find a pentagram revealed. Samhain and Halloween celebrations traditionally incorporate Apples by serving hot spiced Apple cider or wine with sliced Apples and bits of toast floating on top.

Apple has a prominent place in Celtic lore. The Celtic god who guides the dead to the Otherworld is Manannán Mac Lir, who lives on an island called Eamhain Abhlach (Place of Apples). Manannán once appeared at

Tara, the ancient seat of the high kings of Ireland, in the guise of a mysterious warrior, carrying a branch of golden Apples that, when shaken, produced music that made everyone who heard it forget all their troubles. And when King Arthur died, he was ferried across the water to Ynys Afallon, or Ynys Afallach—that is, Avalon, the Isle of Apples.

Druids to this day use a ritual tool called a "bell branch" or "Apple branch," which is a stick of Apple wood with nine bells on it. The bell branch is shaken before a ritual to drive away negative energies and attract helpful fairies (who love the sound of tinkling bells).

The Apple Tree

O apple tree, apple branch,
O apple tree o ho,
Apple tree, flourishing apple tree,
O apple tree o ho.

O apple tree, the Gods be with thee,
May the moon and the sun be with thee,
May the east and west winds be with thee,
May everything that ever existed be with thee,
May every bounty and desire be with thee,
May every passion and divinity be with thee,
May great Somerled* and his band be with thee,
May everyone, like myself, be with thee. . . .

ADAPTED FROM A SCOTTISH TRADITIONAL
WAULKING SONG, AS DESCRIBED BY ALEXANDER
CARMICHAEL IN HIS NINETEENTH-CENTURY
CARMINA GADELICA

The Apple tree has long been valued for its medicinal offerings. Eat peeled raw Apples to stop diarrhea (add some Cinnamon to enhance the effectiveness). Eat whole unpeeled Apples, raw or baked, for a laxative effect.

---

*Regarded as a significant figure in twelfth-century Scottish and Manx history, Somerled is proclaimed as a patrilineal ancestor by several Scottish clans.

Warm baked Apples can be used to poultice a sore throat, on the chest for lung conditions with fever, or on any inflamed area.

The inner bark and bark of the tree's root are used to make a tea (decoction) that you can drink to relieve intermittent fever or use as a wash for mouth sores and sore eyes.

Raw Apple cider is excellent for the digestive system. Take it after a round of antibiotics to bolster intestinal flora. To improve digestion, take it daily. *To make a daily tonic:* Combine 2 teaspoons Apple cider vinegar with 8 ounces water and honey or Maple syrup to taste.

🌰 Spiced Crab Apples*

Here is a dish to serve alongside wild game, lamb, ham, or pork.

> 1½ pounds organic or wild-harvested crab apples
>
> 1¼ cups organic apple cider vinegar
>
> 3 cups organic sugar
>
> 1 teaspoon organic ground cinnamon
>
> ½ teaspoon organic ground ginger
>
> ¼ teaspoon organic ground cloves

Wash the crab apples and cut them in half.

Combine the vinegar and sugar in a pan over medium heat and simmer until the sugar is dissolved. Add the spices and crab apples to the pan. Simmer until the apples are soft but unbroken.

Lift the apples out with a perforated spoon and transfer to clean, warm, dry jars.

Boil the syrup left in the pan until it is reduced by half. Pour the syrup over the crab apples. Seal the jars. Once processed in a boiling water bath and sealed, the fruits should last about 12 to 18 months, if not sealed then keep in the refrigerator for about a week.

---

*Adapted from Pamela Michael, *A Country Harvest* (New York: Exeter Books, 1987), 111.

> **CAUTION: Apple seeds contain cyanide. A large number of them (about a cupful) could kill an adult. Also, Apple juice has a lot of sugar, and diabetics should use it with caution.**

Apple Tree at Samhain

At midnight on Samhain, to divine the initials of your next lover, throw freshly peeled Apple parings over your shoulder and see what letter they form. Hold an Apple in your hand until it is warm and then hand it to your intended; if they bite into it, they are yours.

The custom of bobbing for Apples at Samhain has Otherworldly connotations; for the ancient Celts, water was the gateway to the fairy realm and the home of the ancestors. Bob for Apples at your Samhain feast after silvering the water with a silver coin (or a piece of silver jewelry) as an offering.

Make yourself a bell branch (see p. 17). Shake it before any Samhain ceremony to ward off negative spirits and attract the fey.

Aspen, Poplar Tree
(Populus balsamifera, P. nigra, P. tremula, P. spp.)

Poplar is a Greek funeral tree sacred to Gaia, the Earth Mother. In ancient Mesopotamia corpses were decorated with golden headdresses fashioned to look like Poplar leaves. Later, in Ireland, the *fe,* or measuring rod used by coffin makers, was traditionally made of Poplar. This "stick of woe" was also used to measure corpses and graves.

Poplar was an ingredient in ancient flying ointments as described in Giambattista della Porta's 1558 *De Miraculis Rerum Naturalium.*

Although they mix in a great deal of superstition, it is apparent nonetheless to the observer that these things can result from a natural force. I shall repeat what I have been told by them. By boiling (a certain fat) in a copper vessel, they get rid of its water, thickening what is left after boiling and remains last. Then they store it, and afterwards boil it again before use: with this, they mix celery, aconite, poplar leaves and soot. Or, in alternative: sium, acorus, cinquefoil, the blood of a bat, nightshade (*Solanum*) and oil; and if they mix in other substances they don't differ from these very much. Then they smear all the parts of the body, first rubbing them to make them ruddy and warm and to rarify whatever had been condensed because of cold. When the flesh is relaxed and the pores opened up, they add the fat (or the oil that is substituted for it)—so that the power of the juices can penetrate further and become stronger and more active, no doubt. And so they think that they are borne through the air on a moonlit night to banquets, music, dances and the embrace of handsome young men of their choice. (Book 2, chapter 26, "Lamiarum Vnguenta" [Witches Unguent])

Today, Poplar is used for protection and to facilitate communication with the dead. You can dry and grind the buds and then combine them with crushed pine resin and rosemary to make an incense to ritually bless and purify an area and keep ill-intentioned ghosts and spirits away. The scent will help in summoning and contacting benevolent spirits too.[4]

Wear a crown of Poplar during rituals for the deceased. Anoint yourself with a Poplar bud salve during rituals to facilitate contact with the dead.

The shaking leaves of Poplar are sensitive to the messages of the gods and spirits. Poplar leaves tremble because of their awareness of the Otherworld and of impending death and calamity. Use this tree to convey messages to the Otherworld by sending your wishes to the wind via the shaking leaves.

> *What earthly hand presumes, aspiring, bold,*
> *The airy harp of ancient bards to hold,*
> *With ivy's sacred wreath to crown his head,*
> *and lead the plaintive chorus of the dead—*
> *He round the poplar's base shall nightly strew*
> *The willow's pointed leaves, of pallid blue,*
> *And still restrain the gaze, reverted keen,*
> *When round him deepen sighs from shapes unseen,*
> *And o'er his lonely head, like summer bees,*
> *The leaves self-moving tremble, on the trees.*
> *When morns first rays fall quivering on the strand,*
> *Then is the time to stretch the daring hand,*

And snatch it from the bending poplar pale,
The magic harp of ancient Teviotdale . . .
FROM "SCENES OF INFANCY" (1803),
BY JOHN LEYDEN

The inner bark (from a twig) and the buds can be taken as tea for fevers, coughs, sore throats, urinary infections, and gonorrhea. Use the buds externally in salves for cuts, scratches, wounds, and burns.

CAUTION: Poplar should be avoided by those who are pregnant or breastfeeding. It can worsen stomach ulcers and bleeding in the stomach and intestines. Do not use Poplar with alcohol, as alcohol may increase the risk of bleeding. People with diabetes, gout, hemophilia, liver disease, or kidney disease should avoid taking Poplar internally.

Poplar Tree at Samhain
Make a crown of Poplar leaves to wear during your ritual. Visit a Poplar tree and tell it your message. When the wind makes the leaves tremble, KNOW that the message has been sent.

Blackthorn
(*Prunus spinosa*)

Dreaming under a Blackthorn tree is said to put you in contact with the fairy realm, but be careful, because this plant is a trickster, both helpful and harmful to humans, according to traditional tales. In one story, a farmer whose grain kept being stolen fell asleep under a Blackthorn, and a voice in his dream told him that the fairies had taken the grain and how to get it back. The farmer succeeded in retrieving the grain, but afterward, it poisoned anyone who ate it.

Blackthorn has a very protective yet fierce and mischievous spirit, the Lunantisidhe (moon fairy), who guards the tree. The Lunantisidhe exits its Blackthorn only on full-moon nights to worship the moon goddess. Cutting a Blackthorn on November 11, Old Samhain Eve, or on May 11,

Old Beltaine Eve, will enrage the Lunantisidhe; it is very dangerous to do so.

Blackthorn was the original barbed wire, making a thick hedge that held in the cattle, and its branches are the traditional wood for shillelaghs, clubs used as a weapon of protection. Witches are said to have wands of Blackthorn to curse with and staffs of Blackthorn for causing mischief and for protection. A staff of Blackthorn is carried at night to keep the fairies away. Keep a stick by the bed for the same purpose.

An old Scottish tale tells the story of William Millar of Cromarty, who explored an underground passage created by fairies and populated by Otherworldly creatures: "Before he entered the cave, Millar sewed sprigs of rowan and witch hazel in the hem of his vest. Into one of his pockets he put a Bible, and in his right hand he held a staff of blackthorn which he had cut on a calm night when the moon was full, and had dressed without using anything made of iron. With the aid of these charms he hoped to be able to protect himself against the spirits of the Under-world."[5]

Notice that Millar made sure not to cut the tree with an iron knife. This is because the fairies despise iron, and even those who are well disposed toward humans will be repelled by an iron knife.

In some parts of Britain, Blackthorn is added to Christmas decorations to bring luck (possibly because its flowers are a herald of spring).

A website devoted to the folklore and traditions of the Irish hedgerow extols the virtues and powers of Blackthorn, noting, "It provides blossom whilst there is still snow on the ground while everything else still seems dead from its winter sleep, its dense branches protect the year's new chicks from predation and in their adulthood provides them with food when many other species of plant have lost their berries." In terms of folklore, we learn that "winter begins when the Cailleach (also the Goddess of Winter) strikes the ground with her Blackthorn staff. . . . [Blackthorn] is often associated with darkness, winter, and the waning or dark moon, [and] a particularly cold spring is referred to as 'a Blackthorn winter.'"[6]

Blackthorn fruits (called sloes) are picked in the fall after one or two frosts, at which point they are made into medicine, used to flavor liqueurs, or eaten in pies, jam, and so on. The dried fruits are added to teas as a flavoring. Sloes are slightly laxative, blood cleansing, and mildly antidiarrheal. The juice of the fresh berries is put on mouth sores and sore throats and used as an astringent styptic to stop bleeding, both internally and externally.

Blackthorn root bark is slightly sedative and can be prepared as a tea for fever. Take the tea on an empty stomach for best effect.

A tea made from Blackthorn flowers is cleansing to the blood, a soothing remedy for skin conditions, and laxative; it also aids digestion.

The leaf tea makes a gargle for sore throats and a wash for sore eyes. Pick the leaves before the summer solstice; after that, they will contain too many alkaloids.

> **CAUTION: Blackthorn seeds contain cyanide, which in tiny amounts can help digestion and respiration but in large amounts can lead to respiratory failure and even death, so please avoid chewing the seeds. This plant may cause birth defects and should be avoided by those who are pregnant or breastfeeding.**
>
> **AND PLEASE NOTE: Blackthorn is considered an invasive species in the United States.**

🍃 Sloe Jelly*

Note that this recipe can be adjusted for any amount of blackthorn fruit you have by using two units of apples for each unit of sloes.

> 1 pound sloes
> 2 pounds apples
> ½ an organic lemon (juice and grated peel)
> 1 pound organic cane sugar per pint of fruit liquid

Measure how many cups of ripe sloes you have, because you will need twice as much apple. Put your sloes into a pot and add just enough water to cover the fruit, bring to a boil, then simmer until the berries are mushy. Mash them up a bit.

Add the washed, chopped organic apples (peel, core, and all). Add the lemon juice and grated peel. Bring to a boil then simmer until everything is pulpy again. Let cool.

---

*Adapted from Andy McKee's "Sloe Jelly Recipe: A Taste of the Wild," Farm in My Pocket (website).

Strain the pulp through a jelly bag, cheesecloth, or fine muslin into a container. For clearer jelly do this very slowly by allowing the pulp to drip overnight.

The next day, measure the liquid and add 1 pound of organic cane sugar per pint. Add a dab of butter to prevent bubbles from forming. Stir over medium heat until it comes to a boil; skim off any scum.

Boil the liquid until it jells when dripped on a cold plate, then ladle into hot jars and seal.

🌿 Sloe Gin*

Pick the sloes on a dry day.

> 4 cups sloes
> 32 ounces (1 quart) gin
> 2¼ cups organic brown sugar
> ½ cup organic white sugar or ¼ cup raw, local honey

Prick each sloe with a knife point, fork tine, or needle and toss into a large bowl or jug. Add the gin and sweeteners and stir well. Pour into a large, very clean glass jar. Cap and allow to steep for 3 months, shaking the jar every few days.

Strain out the gin through cheesecloth several times. Do **not** squeeze the sloes; leave them intact and whole. Bottle the gin and let stand for a year before drinking. The leftover berries can be made into Sloe Gin Jelly, just follow the recipe on page 23!

---

*Adapted from Pamela Michael, *A Country Harvest* (New York: Exeter Books, 1987), 140.

Blackthorn at Samhain

Make a small charm of Blackthorn, or of Rowan, Witch Hazel, and Blackthorn, bound with red thread, to hide in your clothing. Eat sloe jelly or drink sloe gin at your Samhain feast. Sleep or meditate under a Blackthorn tree to contact the fairy realm.

Prick a ripe sloe berry with a quill and use the juice to write a wish, prayer, or petition on Birch bark, linen, or cotton. The ink is indelible. Bury the bark or cloth, burn it, or tie it to a tree that overhangs a water source.

Dandelion
(*Taraxacum officinale*)

Dandelion is used to summon spirits. Use the roots to summon earth deities and fairies who live underground, the leaves to summon the nature spirits and land spirits, and the flowers and seeds to communicate with the goddesses, gods, and sky deities.[7]

Dandelion is widely used as an edible herb. Add the petals (but not the green sepals, which are very bitter) to fritters, salads, and cookies for a calcium boost, or infuse the petals in honey. Add the leaves to stir-fries, salads, and soups. Use the flowers to make Dandelion wine. Dry-roast the roots and chop them up to extend coffee or make a coffee substitute.

🌱 Dandelion Wine*

Gather the blossoms when they are fully open on a sunny day. Remove the bitter green sepals.

> 3 quarts dandelion blossoms (bitter green sepals removed)
> 1 gallon spring water
> 2 organic oranges, with peel
> 1 organic lemon, with peel
> 3 pounds organic sugar or 1½ pounds honey
> 1 5-gram package wine yeast (good for up to 6 gallons of water; the less water you use the faster the wine will ferment)
> 1 pound organic raisins

Put the flowers in a large pot or crock. Bring the water to a boil and pour it over the flowers. Cover and let steep for 3 days.

Shave off the zest of the oranges and lemon, setting aside the interior fruit for the next step. Add the zests to the flower water. Bring to a boil, then remove the zests. Add the sugar or honey, stir until the sweetener is dissolved, and then allow to cool.

Slice the oranges and lemon into thin rounds. Add the citrus slices, yeast, and raisins to the liquid. Put everything into a crock with a loose lid (so gas can escape) to ferment. Stir daily with a wooden spoon or nonreactive stir stick.

---

*Adapted from Laurie Neverman, "Dandelion Wine Recipe—And the Mistake You Don't Want to Make," Common Sense Home (website), April 5, 2018.

After 1 to 2 weeks, when the mixture has stopped bubbling, the ferment is ready. Strain the liquid through several layers of cheesecloth and transfer to sterilized bottles. Slip a deflated balloon over the top of each bottle to monitor for further fermentation. When the balloon remains deflated for 24 hours, fermentation in that bottle is complete. Cork the bottles and store in a cool, dark place for at least 6 months before drinking.

🍂 Dandelion Coffee*

> 25–30 large dandelion roots, scrubbed, washed, and then
> soaked in water with a teaspoon of vinegar or sea salt
> for 20 minutes (to remove parasites)

Rinse and air dry the roots, then cut into 1-inch chips. Dry the roots in a slow oven (about 200 degrees) for an hour. Cut them into very small pieces (about the size of a coffee bean) and spread them on a cookie sheet to bake for another 30 minutes at 220 degrees until very dry and dark brown. Allow them to cool and then grind them in a coffee grinder. Then roast them again at 180 degrees for 5 minutes.

Store in a tin or other airtight container.

To Make the Coffee

Steep 6 tablespoons per 2 cups freshly boiled water for 30 minutes. Strain into a second pot and re-heat before serving. Add cream, honey, and a swizzle of cinnamon stick for extra flair.

Serve hot or iced.

You can also add ground dandelion roots and ground chicory roots (*Cichorium intybus*) to your regular coffee as an extender.

---

*Adapted from Robin Harford's "Dandelion Root Coffee Recipe," *EatWeeds* (blog).

Dandelion root tea is used for acne and eczema and for liver issues. *To make the tea:* Dig up the roots and soak them for 20 minutes in cold water with a little salt or vinegar to remove parasites. Chop the roots. For every 2 teaspoons chopped roots, add ½ cup water. Simmer for about 15 minutes. Take up to 1 cup a day in ¼-cup doses.

A Dandelion libation enhances rituals and celebrations. *To make the libation:* Mix together one part chopped, dry-roasted Dandelion root, two parts honey, and two parts brandy. Allow the mix to steep in a sealed container for at least a month, shaking it every few days. Then strain through a cheesecloth and bottle. Add the liqueur to coffee, tea, cocktails, and other beverages.

> **CAUTION: Dandelion root should be avoided by those who are pregnant or breastfeeding. If you are allergic to Ragweed, you may react to this plant as well.**

Dandelion at Samhain

Stuff a poppet with Dandelion fluff. Gather a dry stalk and blow the seeds as you make a wish. Use a Dandelion libation with coffee, ice cream, or brandy during your Dumb Supper.

Elder
(*Sambucus canadensis, S. nigra*)

In Ireland and on the Isle of Man, Elder was considered a fairy tree, where helpful fairies would play in the Elder branches. For this reason, every house once had an Elder near its door. It was said that if you cut down the tree, the fairies would grieve and leave.

Elder is renowned for the protection it offers against negative forces and spirits. Make a wreath of Elder and place it on the door for protection. Hang bouquets or bags filled with Elder and Wormwood on gates and doors to repel evil spirits and demons.[8] Carry a stick of Elder or a small, equal-armed solar cross made of Elder bound with red thread as a charm against evil.

In the traditional tale "Old Nance and the Buggane" from the Isle of Man, we find evidence of Elder's reputation.

> There was once an old woman living at Laxey, and her name was Nance Corlett. Clean and neat her house was, with the thatch all trim and trig against the winter storms, the tramman (elder) tree by the door, to keep off witches, and the little red cocks and hens wandering in and out of the open door. There wasn't a word going a-speaking against old Nance, in all the Island.[9]

As you know, there are many kinds of fairies. In Scotland these are known as Gude Wichts (Scots language) or "The Seely Court" and Wicked Wichts or "The Unseely Court." Some of them like humans and help around the house and barn, and others seek to do us injury. Wrap a wreath of Elder around the milk churn to protect the milk from ill-intentioned fairies and Witches. In Scotland, hearse drivers made their whips out of Elder wood to guard against ghosts, and it was said that applying the green juice of the leaves to your eyelids while standing under an Elder tree on or near a fairy mound on Samhuinn (Samhain) would enable you to see the fairies. Elder is also considered a Mother Goddess tree, and in Britain sprigs were once placed in the coffin at a funeral or planted near a grave to protect the dead.

Elder has a long history of use in herbal medicine. Elderflower tea opens the pores and promotes sweating, thus lowering a fever. The very young leaves are used in salves for wounds and burns. The ripe berry tea or wine is rich in iron, building to the blood, and a remedy for chest conditions such as bronchitis. The tincture or tea of Elderberries actually blocks the flu virus when taken every 2 hours in hot water or herbal tea.

CAUTION: The ripe berries must be cooked or tinctured; they should not be eaten raw. Elderberries should be avoided by those who are pregnant or breastfeeding and by anyone with an autoimmune condition, like multiple sclerosis (MS), lupus (systemic lupus erythematosus, SLE), rheumatoid arthritis (RA), et cetera.

🍃 Elderberry-Blackberry Jelly*

Elderberry jam is soothing to intestinal irritations. Use ripe elderberries and slightly underripe blackberries. If you freeze the elderberries, they should then easily drop from the stems.

> 2 pounds elderberries
> 2 pounds blackberries

---

*Adapted from Pamela Michael, *A Country Harvest* (New York: Exeter Books, 1987), 181.

Organic sugar

Dab of butter

Combine all the berries in a nonaluminum pot and add just enough cold water to cover them. Bring to a boil and cook for about 15 minutes, mashing with a wooden spoon every few minutes. When the berries are soft and well mashed, transfer the mixture to a jelly bag or cheesecloth bundle to drip into a large bowl overnight.

The next day, measure the juice and pour it into a nonaluminum pot. For every 2½ cups of juice, add 1½ cups sugar. Add a tiny bit of butter to prevent bubbles from forming, then bring to a boil and stir continuously until the sugar is fully dissolved. Keep boiling rapidly for 10 minutes, or until the liquid jells when dripped onto a cold plate. Skim off any bubbles.

Pour the boiling-hot mixture into warm, dry jars and seal.

🍃 Elderberry Sorbet

This would be an elegant dessert for a Samhain Dumb Supper. First you need to make the syrup.

Elderberry Syrup

Elderberries (about half a brown paper lunchbagful makes

about 2 cups)

1 tablespoon sea salt or vinegar

Remove the berries from the stalks and soak them in cold water with a tablespoon of salt or vinegar for 20 minutes to remove any parasites. Rinse the berries.

Pack the berries into a lidded pot and add about ¼ cup of water to just cover the bottom of the pan. Simmer, covered, on low heat for about 12 minutes or until the berries burst. Remove from the stove and mash the berries with a wooden spoon or a potato masher. Drain out the juice through a colander and reserve.

The Sorbet*

2 cups elderberry syrup

1½ cups organic apple juice

---

*Adapted from Rachel Demuth's "Elderberry Sorbet," *Demuths Blog,* August, 26, 2015.

Combine the elderberry syrup and the apple juice. Pour into an ice cream maker and churn until thick. Freeze the sorbet for at least 1 hour to set before serving.

Makes 4 servings.

Elder at Samhain

Place Elder branches above the door or hang a wreath of Elder and Wormwood on your entrances. Make equal-armed solar crosses with Elder twigs and place them around the house or wear them as protective charms.

Balsam Fir (Abies balsamea)
Pine (Pinus spp.)
White Cedar (Thuja occidentalis)

The scent of evergreen Fir, Pine, and White Cedar is said to drive out evil. In Scotland, Halloween torches made of Fir were lit and carried around the borders of the fields in a sunwise (clockwise) direction to "*sain*" (purify) the land. Carry lit Fir or Pine staves into a room to drive out ghosts. Dry and powder Pine or Fir resin and use it as incense to bring peace to an area. Burn Cedar twig tips to purify a house, a ritual area, and the land.

Pine is a traditional tree of choice to make a coffin. Boughs of Pine are often placed on graves, and the needles of Pine and Cedar are burned to comfort the bereaved.

In Scotland, a type of fairy known as Ghillie Dhu (Scottish Gaelic for "dark-haired servant lad") lives in the woodlands and considers himself their guardian. While he generally prefers Birches, he may be seen anywhere there are dense, untouched wild places such as deep forests of Fir and Pine. He is short of stature and likes to disguise himself as foliage. Clothed in leaves and woven moss, he is shy and generally kind to children who have lost their way in the dark, but not so kind to adults. He is most active at night. The Ghillie Dhu were once found all over Scotland, but due to increasing development and tree cutting they are becoming very rare.

Medicinally speaking, Balsam Fir has an antiseptic pitch that can be spread directly on wounds and ulcers. Add about 1 teaspoon of the pitch to a cup of hot water and drink as a tea for bronchitis, cough, sore throat, inflammation of the mucous membranes, colds and flu, diarrhea, earache, vaginal infections, heart problems, rheumatism or inflammation, or pain in the muscles and joints.

CAUTION: Avoid ingesting Balsam Fir, Pine, or White Cedar if you are pregnant or breastfeeding.

The Pine resin that drips down the outer bark has many healing qualities; gather it fresh or dry and use it in salves. Simmer Pine needles and shoots or White Cedar branch tips in water to make a wound wash and an antiseptic, expectorant tea that is very high in vitamin C.

Pine needles and Balsam Fir and White Cedar tips also make an excellent infused oil that can be used for massaging or for any condition where you want to stimulate blood flow. It can help decrease swelling, tenderness, inflammation, and pain within sore muscles or joints. *To make the oil:* Put the plants in a baking dish and add just enough oil to cover them. As a rule, I use cold-pressed organic olive oil, but other oils are also favored by massage therapists, such as almond oil, apricot kernel oil, jojoba oil, coconut oil, and the like. Bake in a very slow oven (about 110°F) for 6 hours, then cool and strain. Use the oil to massage rheumatic pains and the chest in cases of chronic cough. The oil is also a good rub for sciatica, pneumonia, and kidney inflammation and to calm the nerves.

◐ Fir, Pine, or Cedar Cough and Cold Remedy

Fill a small pot with fresh balsam fir, white pine, or white cedar branch tips and just barely cover with fresh, cold water. Cover tightly and simmer (do not boil!) until the water starts to turn brown (at least 20 minutes). Turn off the flame and allow the brew to sit for 2 days. Strain through cheesecloth. Measure the liquid and add about the same volume of honey. Simmer again until the mixture combines thoroughly and then pour the syrup into a clean glass jar while it is still warm. Cap tightly.

The dose is 1 teaspoon of the syrup in a cup of hot tea or hot water. Take as needed for colds, cough, sore throat, and chest complaints.

Fir, Pine, and Cedar at Samhain

Soak a cloth in oil and beeswax and wrap it around a stick of one of these woods to make a torch. *Sain* (purify) the house and land by walking the boundaries in a sunwise (clockwise) direction, carrying the burning or smoking brand.

Seek out a deep, dark Pine or Fir forest. Bring an offering of fruit or flowers and place it under a tree. Sit on the ground and meditate, listening for the sounds of the woodland spirits.

Fumitory
(Fumaria officinalis)

An herb of Saturn used in exorcisms, Fumitory is said to have been created from gases emerging from underground. When burned or used as a wash, it dispels negative energies. Use it to consecrate ritual tools and to purify the home, and burn it in the ritual fire to dispel negative forces. As it drives away bad spirits, Fumitory can build a sense of discipline and spiritual focus.

The Saxon "Nine Herbs Charm"

The "Nine Herbs Charm" is a magical incantation found in the *Lacnunga*, a collection of Anglo-Saxon texts and prayers. The charm, said to have been one of the most powerful healing spells in Anglo-Saxon medicine, calls for combining nine herbs with various other ingredients to make a salve for healing infection and poisoning. Though the identity of some of the herbs, like Mugwort, Plantain, and Nettle, is clear, experts differ as to the identity of, in particular, the herb named as Attorlothe. Some researchers identify this herb as Fumitory, which would make sense, given its powerful healing properties, native range, and long historical use in the intertwined fields of magic and medicine.

As you'll see from the excerpt (translated from Old English) below, the "Nine Herbs Charm" was known to be exceedingly powerful.

> Now these nine herbs have strength
> against nine who have fled from glory,
> against nine poisons and against nine contagions,
> against the red poison, against the dark poison,
> against the white poison, against the pale blue poison,
> against the yellow poison, against the green poison,
> against the dusky poison, against the dark blue poison,
> against the brown poison, against the purple poison,
> against worm-blister, against water-blister,
> against thorn-blister, against thistle-blister,
> against the ice-blister, against the poison-blister,
> if any poison comes flying from the east,
> or any from the north comes,
> or any from the west over the tribe of men . . .
>
> Mugwort, waybread [plantain] which has opened from the east, lamb's cress, attorlothe [betony?, black nightshade?], chamomile, nettle, wood sour apple, chervil and fennel, old soap; work the herbs into powder, mix with the soap and the apple's juice. Make a paste of water and of ash; take the fennel, boil in the paste and warm it with the mixture when he puts on the salve, and before and after. Sing that charm on each of the herbs thrice before he prepares them, and on the apple also, and sing into the mouth of the man and both the ears and on the wound that same charm before he puts on the salve.[10]

The tea and tincture of Fumitory are used internally for eczema, psoriasis, and other skin blemishes; for constipation; for strep throat; as a blood and liver cleanser; and as a remedy for colicky pain affecting the gallbladder and biliary system. It is laxative and diuretic. *To make the tea:* Steep 2 teaspoons Fumitory in 1 cup freshly boiled water for

15 minutes. A 150-pound adult can take up to 3 cups a day. *To make the tincture:* Using the flowering herb, follow the general instructions for making tinctures on pages 8–9. Take a ½ teaspoon in water or tea, 4 times a day, not with meals.

> **CAUTION: Fumitory is a very powerful plant. Use it for no more than a few days. Women who are pregnant or breastfeeding and children should avoid it altogether. Signs of overdose include diarrhea, muscle cramps, and shortness of breath.**

Use Fumitory externally in salves for eczema, psoriasis, and acne. Combine it with young Walnut leaves to poultice wounds, cuts, and abrasions.

Add it to a sitz bath for hemorrhoids. Carefully filter the tea through a coffee filter and apply to the eyes as a wash to relieve conjunctivitis.[11]

Fumitory at Samhain

Make a strong tea and use it to wash your most important magical tools. The spirit of Fumitory will clear away any malevolent forces that impede you so that only the helpful ones appear.

Ivy
(Hedera helix)

Ivy is a go-between for this world and the world of spirits and can show us the future. "Ivy represented peace to the Druids of old, perhaps because of its ability to bind different plants or even different kinds of plants together. Today ivy is often used at weddings, where it symbolizes fidelity."[12]

Bind Ivy with Sweet Woodruff (*Galium odoratum*) or Bramble (*Rubus fruticosus*) and Rowan (*Sorbus aucuparia, S. americana*) into a wreath and hang it on the house or barn to protect animals and people from sorcery and disease.

English Ivy is tinctured in vinegar to treat corns and warts. *To make the vinegar tincture:* Dry the leaves in a very slow oven (110°F for a few hours) and then pack them into a jar. Cover with organic apple cider vinegar, cap, and allow to steep for 2 weeks. Shake the jar daily. Strain and keep in a cool, dark place. Apply the vinegar tincture on a cloth as a poultice, 1 hour a day, until relief is experienced.

English Ivy can be also be used in salves for burns.* (Follow the instructions on page 7 to make the salve.)

The tea of English Ivy leaves makes an external wash for ulcers, wounds, burns, boils, dandruff, and skin irritations, a douche for vaginitis, and a tea for bilious complaints and mucousy lung conditions.

> CAUTION: Ivy should not be used for more than 20 days, and women who are pregnant or breastfeeding should avoid internal use. Some people may experience mild stomach upset or contact dermatitis from this plant.

Ivy at Samhain

Use long strands of Ivy to bind a wreath of protective herbs, and hang the wreath on your door. On Samhain Eve, pin three leaves of Ivy onto your nightshirt or nightgown to dream of your future lover.

Juniper, Mountain Yew
(Juniperus communis)

In Celtic tradition, Juniper and Rowan are placed over the door at Beltaine and Samhain to protect the house from sorcery on these potent spirit nights. In Wales, it is said that if you cut one down, you will be dead within the year, and for this reason aged Junipers are always left to die a natural death. In England, juniper is burned in the house to repulse sorcerers, and the smoke is also said to keep away serpents and disease.

Burn Juniper branches before the entrance to the house and barn and

---

*Other herbs to consider for burns are Comfrey (*Symphytum officinale*), Bee Balm (*Monarda* spp.), Horse Chestnut (*Aesculus hippocastanum*), and Aloe (*Aloe vera*). If you happen to have any of these, you can use them in combination with English Ivy to make the salve.

in the hearth on New Year's morning as an act of ritual purification. The tips of the branches can be burned all year to bring peace and harmony to the home.

Carry a bit of Juniper wood on your travels; you can shave off a bit and burn it to drive away evil. The dried berries can be worn or burned for protection too, as seen in the ancient Navajo magical practice of gathering "ghost beads"—Juniper berries that have fallen to the ground, been eaten and hollowed out by ants, and then dried naturally by the sun.

> The dried berries are strung together with beads to create ghost necklaces that are believed to bring peace and protection to the wearer. Ghost bead necklaces are also believed to ward off evil spirits and negative energy, as well as protect the wearer from nightmares. . . . Another common belief surrounding ghost beads is that the beads kept the spirits happy when the Navajos entered the ruins.[13]

A tea of the berries helps chest congestion and edema. It is also a urinary antiseptic for cystitis, catarrh of the bladder, weak digestion, and gas.

CAUTION: Avoid Juniper berries if you have weak kidneys or if you are pregnant or breastfeeding. No one should take the berry tea for more than 2 weeks. Long-term use or overuse of Juniper may dramatically lower blood sugar levels or make some stomach and bowel irritations worse, and Juniper may unpredictably affect blood pressure, either raising it or lowering it.

The infused oil of Juniper can be used in massage for rheumatism and arthritis. *To make the oil:* Just barely cover the berries and branch tips with oil and bake in very slow oven (110°F) for about 6 hours. Strain, bottle, and store in a cool, dark location.

The Navajo use Juniper wood ash in the traditional dish of blue corn mush; the ash is an alkalinizer that helps break down the corn and reduce the cooking time. As it turns out, the ash is also a good source of calcium, and so it helped the Navajo, who as a culture tend to be lactose-intolerant, meet their nutritional needs.[14]

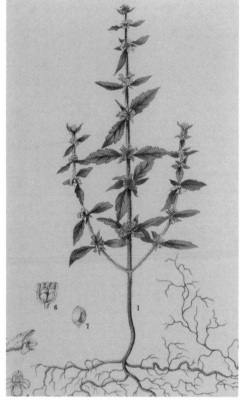

Plate 1 (left). Aconite, Monkshood, Wolfsbane (*Aconitum napellus*)

Plate 2 (right). American, or "False," Pennyroyal (*Hedeoma pulegioides*)

Plate 3. Apple Tree (*Malus* spp.)

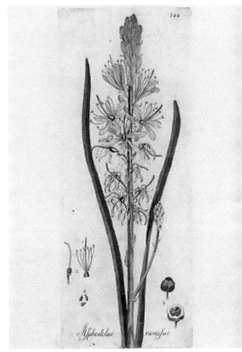

Plate 4 (left). Aspen, Poplar Tree
(*Populus balsamifera, P. nigra,
P. tremula, P.* spp.)

Plate 5 (right). Asphodel
(*Asphodelus ramosus*)

Plate 6. Basil (*Ocimum basilicum*),
Holy Basil, Tulsi (*Ocimum tenuiflorum*)

Plate 7 (left). Balsam Fir
(*Abies balsamea*)

Plate 8 (right). Belladonna, Deadly
Nightshade (*Atropa belladonna*)

Plate 9. Black Fava Beans
(*Vicia faba*)

Plate 10 (left). Blackthorn
(*Prunus spinosa*)

Plate 11 (right). Blue Lotus
(*Nymphaea caerulea*)

Plate 12. Cannabis
(*Cannabis sativa, C. indica,
C. ruderalis*)

ate 13. Carrageen (*Chondrus crispus*)

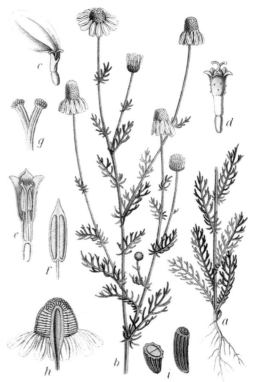

Plate 14. Chamomile
(*Matricaria recutita, Chamaemelum nobile*)

Plate 15. Chervil
(*Myrrhis odorata*)

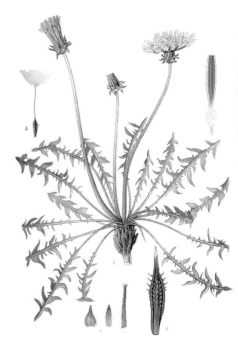

Plates 16 and 17. Dandelion
(*Taraxacum officinale*)

Plate 18. Dittany of Crete
(*Origanum dictamnus*)

Plate 19. Elder
(*Sambucus canadensis, S. nigra*)

Plate 20 (left). Fumitory
(*Fumaria officinalis*)

Plates 21 (top right) and 22 (bottom).
Hawthorn, May Tree, Whitethorn
(*Crataegus* spp.)

Plate 23 (left). Hazel (*Corylus avellana*)
Plate 24 (right). Ivy (*Hedera helix*)

Plate 25. Juniper, Mountain Yew
(*Juniperus communis*)

Juniper at Samhain

Make a necklace of dried Juniper berries. Burn Juniper in the hearth to purify your home.

Lichens

Lichens grow on rocks, trees, and other solid surfaces. They are "plant-like" organisms, hosting symbiotic relationships between fungi and chlorophyll-producing algae. They range in color from green to gray to brown, sometimes with brightly colored spots. In the Celtic tradition, any red spots you might see on a lichen are said to be fairy blood—clear evidence that the local fairies have been getting into fights and other mischief, as they tend to do on Samhain Eve (any spot where fairy battles have been seen to occur would be a good location to keep an eye out for them).

The following Native American legend provides another explanation for lichen.

The Okanagan-Colville have a legend about how *Bryoria fremontii* was created. The lichen is said to have originated from Coyote's hair. There are several variants of this legend. In one variation, Coyote tries to catch some swans but they end up flying away with him and only letting go when he is high up in the air. Coyote falls and becomes caught in the branches of a tree. When Coyote is finally able to free himself, he leaves much of his hair entangled in the branches. Coyote then transformed this hair into *Bryoria fremontii,* saying, "You, my hair, will not be wasted. The coming people will gather you and make you into food." And the lichen has been used as food ever since.[15]

Lichens contain powerful antibiotic substances and are also immune building. In particular, Lichens are effective against gram-positive bacteria, such as *Streptococcus, Staphylococcus, Mycobacterium tuberculosis,* and other fast-growing species. They don't seem to work for gram-negative bacteria such as *Salmonella* and *Escherichia coli.*[16]

Usnea spp. (Bearded Lichen) is used for urinary tract and upper respiratory infections. Chinese herbalists use *Usnea longissima* as a powder on infected ulcers. The ancient Greeks most likely used *Usnea barbata* for uterine infections. *Lobaria pulmonaria* (Lungwort) is simmered in milk to make a tea for coughs. *Cetraria islandica* (Iceland Moss) has been used traditionally for respiratory, urinary, and digestive issues. Scandinavians mix it into breads, gruel, and porridge or make it into lemon-, ginger-, or cinnamon-flavored gelatin for the sick.

Cautions: *Usnea* **spp. should be avoided by women who are pregnant or breastfeeding and anyone with liver disease. Long-term use could harm the liver. Lungwort should be avoided by women who are pregnant or breastfeeding. Iceland Moss should be avoided by women who are pregnant or breastfeeding and anyone with stomach or intestinal ulcers.**

Lichen at Samhain

Scope out a Lichen-covered rock and return to it after Samhain to see if the fairies have had a battle.

Maidenhair Spleenwort
(*Asplenium trichomanes*)

The fairies hide the entrance to their hills with luxuriant growths of ferns such as Spleenwort. On Samhain night, the ferns part as the fairies emerge on their travels. Watch for them and begin a relationship.

> *Where the wandering water gushes*
> *From the hills above Glen-Car,*
> *In pools among the rushes,*
> *That scarce could bathe a star,*
> *We seek for slumbering trout,*
> *And whispering in their ears*
> *We give them evil dreams,*
> *Leaning softly out*
> *From ferns that drop their tears*
> *Of dew on the young streams.*

Come, O human child!
To the woods and waters wild,
With a fairy, hand in hand,
For the world's more full of weeping than you can
  understand.

FROM "THE STOLEN CHILD" (1889), BY W. B. YEATS

Make an infusion of Spleenwort leaves for coughs, tuberculosis, and insomnia.

To make the tea: Steep 1 ounce of the leaf per pint of freshly boiled water for 20 minutes. Take in 3 tablespoons doses and add raw, local honey for a cough.

CAUTION: Avoid Spleenwort during pregnancy. Using large amounts for a long period of time could lead to a vitamin B deficiency.

Ferns at Samhain

On Samhain Eve, keep an eye on your ferns and see if they part as the fairies emerge. Leave a dish of food near a lush stand of ferns for the fairies' enjoyment.

Mandrake
(Mandragora officinarum, M. autumnalis)

Ancient Egyptian paintings sometimes show priest-shamans guiding the living and the dead, accompanied by both Mandrake and sacred Blue Lotus (*Nymphaea caerulea*). (Blue Lotus is aphrodisiac, euphoriant, and slightly mind altering and helps alleviate pain. The flowers are brewed as tea or soaked in wine.)

In modern traditions, Mandrake protects against demonic possession and is used in exorcisms. To activate a root, first display it prominently in the home for three days and then soak it in water overnight. Sprinkle the water on entrances, windows, and people. Left on the mantel, it attracts prosperity and happiness to the house.

According to ancient tradition, when digging up the root you should avoid touching it, because the first person to do so will likely die (this is why dogs were once used to pull it from the earth). I think this is just another way of saying that the plant needs to be respected because those who misuse it could even end up dead! Mandrake roots are used as poppets for good or ill. To make a poppet, take a root that looks like a person, decorate it to make it more closely resemble your "target," and then focus blessings or curses on the homunculus.

Mandrake was a common ingredient in witches' flying ointments.

In De Prestaegeous Demonium (1563) . . . the German physician and demonologist Johann Weyer made explicit connections between witches and plants of the nightshade family like henbane, mandrake, and datura. . . . Belladonna, along with other plants of the nightshade family like mandrake, henbane, and datura are believed to have been an ingredient in witch ointment, spread on the skin by certain individuals to produce vivid dreams, magical flights of fancy, or trance-like states.[17]

Not poppy, nor mandragora,
Nor all the drowsy syrups of the world,
Shall ever medicine thee to that sweet sleep
Which thou owdst yesterday.

FROM *OTHELLO*, ACT 3, SCENE 3,
BY WILLIAM SHAKESPEARE

Oblivion I can give you. Mystic drops of a magic herb I know that renews the heart. But whoever wants it must gather it with his own hand at the dead of night—the graveyard is the place. To the west of the city, there, where on the gloomy field the pallid moon shines down on abhorrent land the herb has its roots by those ill-famed stones where all sins are atoned for with the last living breath!

GIUSEPPE VERDI,
UN BALLO IN MASCHERA, ACT 1, SCENE 2

The ancient Greeks considered Mandrake to be an aphrodisiac. They also used it to help with insomnia, anxiety, and depression and as a general pain remedy. For these purposes they soaked the root in sour wine (using about ⅓ cup of fresh or dried root per liter of wine) and allowed it to steep for about a week.

Mandrake root can be added to skin-healing salves. The fresh leaves can be chewed to relieve toothache and the dried leaves burned and inhaled to allay coughs and headaches.

Tincture the root in brandy to make a remedy for rheumatic pain or in wine to bestow sleep. The dose is 10 or fewer drops at a time (assuming a 150-pound adult).

> **CAUTION: Mandrake should not be taken internally more than once a week, and larger doses could be fatal. Mandrake should be avoided by women who are pregnant or breastfeeding, children, those with Down's syndrome, the elderly, and anyone with heart disease, liver problems, kidney problems, high blood pressure, overactive thyroid, myasthenia gravis, enlarged prostate, problems with urination, heartburn, GERD, hiatal hernia, stomach ulcers, ulcerative colitis, or other serious digestive disorders. Also note that Mandrake contains trance-inducing tropane alkaloids.**

Mandrake at Samhain

Display a Mandrake root in your home for three days: the day before Samhain, the day of Samhain, and the day after. Then soak it in water overnight and use the water to sprinkle entrances, exits, and windows. Leave the root on display afterward.

Mistletoe
(Viscum album)

Mistletoe grows on trees such as Apples and Poplars, but the ancient Druids celebrated when they found Mistletoe growing on Oak, I believe because they knew it had the most potent curative value (and modern studies have confirmed this). In fact, anthroposophical medicine uses a remedy called Iscador, made from Mistletoe found growing on Oak, for cancerous tumors.

Pliny the Elder wrote the following account of Druids and Mistletoe.

> Upon this occasion we must not omit to mention the admiration that is lavished upon this plant by the Gauls. The Druids—for that is the name they give to their magicians—held nothing more sacred than the mistletoe and the tree that bears it, supposing always that tree to be the robur.* Of itself the robur is selected by them to form whole groves, and they perform none of their religious rites without employing branches of it; so much so, that it is very probable that the priests themselves may have received their name from the Greek name for that tree. In fact, it is the notion with them that everything that grows on it has been sent immediately from heaven, and that the mistletoe upon it is a proof that the tree has been selected by God himself as an object of his especial favour.
>
> The mistletoe, however, is but rarely found upon the robur; and when found, is gathered with rites replete with religious awe. This is done more particularly on the fifth day of the moon, the day which is the beginning of their months and years, as also of their ages, which, with them, are but thirty years. This day they select because the moon, though not yet in the middle of her course, has already considerable power and influence; and they call her by a name which signifies, in their language, the all-healing. Having made all due preparation for the sacrifice and a banquet beneath the trees, they bring thither two white bulls, the horns of which are bound then for the first time. Clad in a white robe the priest ascends the tree, and cuts the mistletoe with a golden sickle, which is received by others in a white cloak. They then immolate the victims, offering up their prayers that God will render this gift of his propitious to those to whom he has so granted it. It is the belief with them that the mistle-

---

*Robur is a name for Oak.

toe, taken in drink, will impart fecundity to all animals that are barren, and that it is an antidote for all poisons.[18]

European Mistletoe stems and leaves are used for fevers and cancer. Mistletoe will also alleviate the symptoms of neurological Lyme disease, though it will not cure it, as it does not kill the spirochetes. It also helps with epilepsy, convulsions, nervous conditions, internal bleeding, and very high fevers such as from typhoid. Mistletoe lowers blood pressure and slows the pulse. It also builds the immune system and is antitumoral.

CAUTION: Make sure you are using twigs and leaves of European Mistletoe (*Viscum album*) and not the American varieties, which are poisonous and abortive. Avoid the berries; they are poisonous in *all species*. Mistletoe should be avoided by those with autoimmune conditions like multiple sclerosis (MS), lupus (systemic lupus erythematosus, SLE), and rheumatoid arthritis (RA), those with heart disease, leukemia, or liver disease, and by anyone who will soon be having surgery or has undergone organ transplant.

Mistletoe at Samhain

Mistletoe enhances any magical spell—use a bit in your charm bag, medicine bundle, or mojo bag.

Cut a sprig of Mistletoe on Samhain Eve, using a new dirk (knife), after walking around the tree sunwise (clockwise) three times. Use the sprig as a charm against sorcery and to bring luck in battle. Or place it under a baby's cradle or mattress to prevent abduction by fairies (please make sure the baby can't reach it).

Mullein
(*Verbascum thapsus*)

Powdered Mullein leaf is used as a substitute for graveyard dust in old grimoires. In India, Mullein is burned to drive away evil spirits. In

Europe, it is used to invoke the fire element in rituals, and "hag's tapers" are made by dipping the flower heads of the dried stalks in a mixture that is half suet and half beeswax and then allowing these "torches" to dry.*

Herbalist Crystal Aneira offers a good description of Mullein's uses in the New World.

> In Great Britain it was used to help bring back children who had been kidnapped by fairies. Various Native Americans knew a good thing when they saw it and used this Eurasian native that became naturalized in North America to return people to their right mind. For instance, the Hopi mixed the leaves with onosmodium† to be used as a smoke by crazy people and those who had been bewitched. The Navajo wrapped the leaves in a corn husk to be smoked to help a mind return if it was lost, and the Potowatami smudged unconscious people with the leaves to help them return to consciousness. Consider mullein useful in centering the spirit and add it to the pipe smoked as an aid to astral work.[19]

Mullein leaf tea is used for bronchitis, especially where there is thick, stubborn mucus, and a tea of the flowers is used as a sleep aid. The leaf poultice is placed on wounds and sores.

Mullein flower oil is an old remedy for earaches and itching in the ears. *To make the oil:* Gather fresh Mullein flowers and place them in a brown or blue glass jar. Add enough olive oil to cover the flowers completely, cap the jar, and place in the hot sun for 3 weeks. The flowers will rot inside the jar, forming their own preservative. Strain the oil and bottle. When needed, pour out a teaspoon of the oil and warm it by holding it briefly over a candle. Test the oil to make sure it isn't too hot, then place it inside the ear. Pack the ear with cotton and leave the oil and cotton in overnight.

---

*For more detailed information on making hag's tapers, see my book *Secret Medicines from Your Garden* (Healing Arts Press, 2016).
†The "onosmodium" she refers to is *Onosmodium bejariense* var. *occidentale,* also known as False Gromwell.

Dried Mullein leaves can be smoked in a pipe or scattered on a hot plate and the smoke inhaled to relieve asthma, coughs, and colds. But a tea—especially when mixed with Sage (*Salvia officinalis*) for a wet cough—is better for the lungs. Add dry Mullein leaves to herbal smoking mixtures for those who are weaning themselves off the tobacco habit.

CAUTION: Women who are pregnant or breastfeeding should avoid Mullein. Children should not use Mullein oil as an earache remedy for more than 3 days.

Mullein at Samhain
Make hag's tapers at least a week before the festival and allow them to dry. Light the way to your Samhain bonfire with them. Burn dried Mullein leaves as incense and inhale the smoke to facilitate contact with the astral or fairy realm.

Nettles
(*Urtica* spp.)

Fresh nettles should be gathered in the spring while wearing rubber or leather gloves and long sleeves. If you rinse the leaves for just a few seconds under cold water, all traces of the "sting" will disappear.

Suspend bunches of Nettles above doorways and hide them under the eaves to ward off evil ghosts and spirits. Hang bunches of Nettles in cloth bags on gateposts and in and around crops to protect them from blight, disease, ill-intentioned spirits, and other noxious influences.[20]

Making Nettle Cloth
In ancient times Nettles were made into a kind of cloth, called ramie. Start by gathering long stems and removing the leaves. (Add the mineral-rich leaves to your compost pile.) Soak the stems in water for 7 to 10 days, pouring off the water every day and replacing it with fresh water. (Use the poured-off water to nourish your house and garden

plants.) Split and dry the stalks and remove the pith by squeezing the stalks flat and running a fingernail up the length of each stalk. Pull off the bark by bending the dry stalk over your fingers. Card and spin the Nettle bark fibers. Weave into cloth.

The following is blogger Leimomi Oakes's retelling of the fairytale "The Wild Swans," about a girl whose brothers are enchanted and turned into swans.

> In order to free them from their spell, our heroine must make each of them a shirt of stinging nettles: and while she spins and sews (or knits, depending on the version), she cannot speak.
>
> Some of the local villagers are suspicious of the silent girl who gathers prickly weeds, and of the garments she is creating. When, desperate for a new source of nettles, she gathers them from the churchyard, the villagers turn against her completely, and try her as a witch. She desperately sews even as they tie her to a stake and pile the wood around her.
>
> As they light the fire, her swan brothers fly overhead and circle around her, and she throws the shirts over them. Unfortunately, she hasn't quite finished the sleeve of the last shirt, so her youngest brother retains his wings.
>
> With her brothers finally freed from the spell, our heroine can finally speak and explain why she was making stinging nettle shirts. The villagers are apologetic, and everyone lives happily ever after (presumably).[21]

Nettles are antihistaminic and a nice alternative to allergy medications. They are warming to the body and will help alleviate rheumatic complaints. As a tea, they will clean the kidneys, help with chest congestion, and both clean and build blood. *To make the tea:* Steep 3 tablespoons chopped Nettles (fresh or dry) for 3 to 10 minutes in a cup of freshly boiled water.

Nettles are very nutritious and full of minerals. In spring, fresh

Nettles can be added to soups, sautéed with other vegetables, folded into omelets, and so on. Try baking them into a pie or adding them to quiche. Nettle broth is a cleansing and warming drink in early spring. I like to gather Nettles, rinse them, dry them in a very slow oven (110°F for several hours), and then crumble them into a jar. I add a teaspoon to soups, stews, and other dishes for a mineral boost all year.

> CAUTION: Do not eat Nettles raw. Avoid Nettles if you are pregnant, as they could cause a miscarriage. Diabetics should monitor their blood sugar levels carefully, as this plant can cause it to rise. Nettles may lower blood pressure and increase urine flow; use with caution if you have severe kidney problems. Do not take Nettles if you have dry scalp, dry eczema, or dandruff.

Nettles at Samhain

Find long, tough Nettle stalks and place them over doorways and on gateposts to protect the home from evil spirits, blight, and disease.

A tenet of natural magic is that courtship is always most successful when carried out by moonlight. Gather Nettles on Samhain Eve, remove the hot, prickly sting by rinsing, dry them, and hide them between the blankets of your intended to gain their love.

Oak Tree
(*Quercus* spp.)

Scottish Highlanders used a stick of Oak to draw a circle around themselves as protection from fairies. In the Irish tale of Diarmad and Grainne, the fleeing lovers stop in an Oak forest and Diarmad cuts seven "doors" of wood to make a magical fence that the pursuing Fianna cannot pass.

Oak is a being that is perfectly balanced between the worlds. Its roots extend as far down as its branches are high. Like Rowan twigs, Oak twigs can be bound with red thread into an equal-armed solar cross and carried or worn to bring protection and balance. Acorns can be carried or worn to promote creativity and conception. Druids were known to carry Acorns (and Hazelnuts) on their person for inspiration and protection.

Oak is a tree of the sun and sacred to the high gods Athena, Hermes, Jupiter, Odin, Perkūnas, Perun, Rhea, Thor, Zeus, Brighid, and the Daghda. Dried and powdered Oak bark can be burned to bring divine assistance from these gods, and Oak logs are appropriate for a ritual fire.

A guardian spirit lives inside each Oak tree. Many have seen it as an old man with a long beard, while others perceive it as a "dryad," or female entity. Each Oak is a doorway to the Otherworld. Druids enter the Oak shamanically by visualizing an opening at the base. From there Druids can travel down via the roots to the Underworld of the sidhe (fairies) and the ancestors, or up via the branches to the Sky World of the gods.

Can a Druid Practice Shamanism?

You may find it strange to consider that Druids might describe their practice as "shamanic." But shamanism is not specific to any particular culture or spiritual practice. I was recently privileged to meet a Mongolian shaman in person. I was teaching at an herb gathering in New Hampshire, and she happened to be visiting the area and did a traditional milk blessing for the assembled herbalists, dancing and spraying mare's milk on the ground while keeping her face covered by a cloth. She said that her face had to be hidden because when she was in trance, it wasn't she who was bestowing the blessing, but rather the ancestors, who were working through her.

When she was finished, I sought her out so we could speak privately. I told her that many Americans are loathe to use the word *shaman* to describe their activities because to do so seems like cultural misappropriation. I asked her what word we Americans could use that would be appropriate and respectful.

Her reply was that we should go ahead and use the word *shaman* because it just means "awakening person." As long as we keep learning and growing and using plants to communicate with the spirits and to heal ourselves and others, we are doing shamanic work.

All kinds of Oaks have external applications as medicine, but the inner bark (the living layer of tissue just under the dead outer bark) of White Oak (*Quercus alba*) is the one for internal use. Gather the bark from a White Oak twig (not the trunk, or you will kill the tree) or from the root of a fallen tree. The inner bark makes a tea for wet coughs in which there is a lot of phlegm, a remedy for diarrhea, and a gargle for sore throats. *To make the tea:* Simply peel off the dead outer bark and then simmer the inner bark (the cambium) for about 20 minutes in a pot with a tight lid, using about 2 teaspoons of inner bark per cup of water.

CAUTION: Do not take White Oak tea for more than 3 days or diarrhea, stomach problems, or intestinal problems could result. Persons with heart conditions, hypertonia, kidney or liver problems, high fever, or infection should avoid it.

Do not use oak bark on the skin for more than 2 to 3 weeks, and do not use it on very large wounds or large patches of eczema. Women who are pregnant or breastfeeding should avoid it.

The leaves and inner bark of other Oak species can be gathered in early spring (do not use the leaves after the summer solstice, as they will contain too many harsh alkaloids) to make a wound wash, douche, and healing salves.

Oak at Samhain

Make tiny solar crosses of Oak twigs bound with red thread and place them in windows or wear them. Gather Acorns and put them in every coat pocket. Place Acorns on the altar. Make an Acorn cake for your Dumb Supper. Meditate under an Oak tree and enter it, rising upward through the trunk to the branches to visit the Sky World of the gods, or go down through the roots to the sidhe realm. Burn Oak in the ritual fire and on the altar to contact the high gods of the Indo-European pantheons.

Pennyroyal (*Mentha pulegium*)
American or "False" Pennyroyal (*Hedeoma pulegioides*)

Pennyroyal is an herb of protection against evil spirits. Keep it in a bowl in the house to bring peace. The tea and oil are used to bathe a corpse and bring them to a peaceful transition to their next life.

How to Avoid the Black Death

Here are some tongue-in-cheek yet highly practical fourteenth-century recommendations for avoiding the plague. As you'll see, Pennyroyal played a big role in medieval survival strategies.

1. Keep some clean clothes tightly folded and bound up in cloth treated with mint or pennyroyal, preferably in a cedar chest far from all animals and vermin.
2. At the first whisper of plague in the area, flee any populated town or village and head for an isolated villa, far from any trade routes, with your cedar chest.
3. Vigilantly clean every last corner of your villa, killing all rats and burning their corpses.
4. Use plenty of mint or pennyroyal to discourage fleas, and allow no cats or dogs to come near you.
5. Once away from all human contact, wash in extremely hot water, change into your clean clothes, and burn the clothes you traveled in.
6. Keep a minimum distance of 25 feet from any other human being to avoid catching any pneumonic form spread through breathing and sneezing.
7. Bathe in hot water as frequently as you can.
8. Keep a fire burning in your villa to ward off the bacillus, and stay as close to it as you can stand, even in summer.
9. Have your armies burn and raze to the ground any nearby houses where plague victims have resided.
10. Pray to the deity or the saint of your choice frequently and fervently.
11. Stay where you are until 6 months after the most recent nearby outbreak.
12. Move to Bohemia before 1347 and don't leave until after 1353.[22]

Pennyroyal leaf tea is a classic for menstrual problems; it "brings on" the period and may cause abortion. The leaf tea is also used for colds.

The essential oil can be rubbed directly on the abdomen to relieve cramps. Mix the oil with oil of Citronella (*Cymbopogon nardus*) to make an effective mosquito repellent that can be rubbed onto the skin.

Tincture the plant in vinegar to make a wash for ulcers, burns, and bruises.

> **CAUTION: Pennyroyal is unsafe for children, for women who are pregnant or breastfeeding, and for those with kidney or liver disease. Do not use Pennyroyal tincture (the alcohol extract) for more than 2 weeks; doing so could be fatal. Pennyroyal should not be used repeatedly or for long periods on the skin—even animals have been harmed by it. If you are making an insecticide, it should not contain more than 1 percent Pennyroyal oil. Be safe and apply it to your hat or clothing, rather than directly to your skin.**
>
> **Pennyroyal oil should not be ingested; it can cause kidney and liver damage, abortion, and even death. Citronella oil can be fatal to children if swallowed.**

Pennyroyal at Samhain

Place a bowl of Pennyroyal on the altar or somewhere in the house to attract kindly spirits.

Pumpkin (*Cucurbita pepo*)
Rutabaga (*Brassica napus napobrassica*)
Turnip (*Brassica rapa rapifera*)

The ancient Celts did not have Pumpkins, which are a Native American vegetable; they carved Rutabagas and Turnips on Samhain, placing a candle inside to illuminate them. For the Celts, the soul of a person was in the head and no enemy could be vanquished fully unless you took their head. Jack-o'-lanterns were lit to frighten away enemies, to honor the spirits of deceased ancestors, and to repel evil and harm from the home.

In these times the Celts still practiced the ritualized beheading of enemies, and these [grisly] trophies would be placed on their door jambs to represent the departed. During the Christian era this tradition persisted with the ornamentation of carved turnips, eventually being turned into lanterns with macabre expressions. Believing that the head was the most powerful part of the body, containing the spirit and the knowledge, the Celts used the "head" of the vegetable to frighten off any spirits wishing to do harm.[23]

Pumpkin seeds are a good remedy for worms. *To prepare the seeds:* Soak the raw seeds overnight, blend them with water, and strain out the Pumpkin seed "milk." Drink the milk and eat more Pumpkin seeds on an empty stomach. Follow with a dose of Castor oil 3 hours later to encourage your body to pass the worms.

Pumpkin seeds are also beneficial to the male reproductive tract. And eating Rutabagas and Turnips in the fall brings resistance to disease at the change of season.

CAUTION: There is some evidence that eating turnips could worsen ulcerative colitis.

Pumpkins, Rutabagas, and Turnips at Samhain

Hollow them out, carve faces into them, put an inch or so of sand in the bottom, and place a candle inside. Arrange them decoratively around the outside of the house. On Samhain Eve, light the candles and place the jack-o'-lanterns in the windows and by the door to welcome your wandering dead.

Rowan Tree, Mountain Ash
(*Sorbus americana, S. aucuparia*)

A fire of Rowan twigs is lit at the entrance to the barn on Samhain and Beltaine to repel evil sorcery. Equal-armed solar crosses of Rowan wood, bound with red thread, are hung in the barn thatch, placed before the door, and hung inside to protect the animals.

A bit of Rowan can be tied to a cow or horse's tail and a wreath of Rowan placed about their neck to ward off misfortune.

Highland women once wore necklaces of Rowan berries as a form of magical protection. Hiding a small equal-armed solar cross of Rowan bound with red thread in your clothes was said to bring protection from ill-intentioned sorcery, ghosts, spirits, and pixies.

The combination of herbs knotted with red thread was an ancient tradition for sealing a magic spell. As the old Scottish saying goes, "Rowan tree and red thread gar [makes] the Witches tyne [lose] their speed."

Wear a crown and necklace of Rowan berries when you summon the spirits. Make a Rowan staff or wand and carry it with you on dark nights. Use a wooden Rowan blade instead of a metal athame in your rites (as everyone knows, the fairies despise iron).

> *O rowan tree!*
>
> *We sat aneath thy spreading shade,*
> *The bairnies [little children] round thee ran,*
> *They pu'd [pulled] thy bonny berries red,*
> *And necklaces they strang.*
> *My mother! O I see her still,*
> *She smil'd our sports to see,*
> *Wi' little Jeanie on her lap,*
> *And Jamie at her knee.*
> *O rowan tree!*
>
> FROM "THE ROWAN TREE" (1822),
> BY CAROLINA OLIPHANT

Rowan berries are ready to harvest after the first frost when they are deep orange (American variety) or red (European variety). You can freeze the ripe berries for later use all winter. Cook the ripe berries into cakes and breads and add them to mead. (Use just a few—they are quite bitter!)

The berries also make powerful medicine. Add a teaspoonful of the juice of the ripe berries to a cup of water to make a gargle for sore throats. Or just barely cover the ripe berries with cold water, simmer for about 20 minutes, and strain out the liquid to make the gargle. The fresh juice is also slightly laxative.

Rowan berry tea is helpful for kidney disease, diabetes, arthritis, vitamin C deficiency, diarrhea, and menstrual problems. It boosts the immune system and strengthens the lungs. *To make the tea:* Soak 1 teaspoon of dried berries per 1 cup of water for 10 hours. Take a ¼ cup 4 times a day, not with meals.

Make a syrup of the berries with slices of apple and honey to treat colds and sore throats. Make the berries into a jam with apples and honey to treat diarrhea in adults and children. The jam is also a tasty condiment to serve with lamb, venison, or cheese.

🌱 Rowan Berry Jam

> 1 part ripe berries (gathered after the first frost)
> 1 part organic apples peeled, cored, and quartered
> ½ part organic cane sugar (or ¼ part raw, local honey)

Place the berries and apples into a pot and barely cover them with water. Bring to a boil. Then turn down the heat and simmer for about 20 minutes or until the berries are soft.

Line a colander with cheesecloth or muslin and pour the berry and apple mixture into it. For clear jelly do not press the fruit through the cloth, for a thicker Jam press the fruit. Allow the liquid to drip into a container overnight, measure the liquid, then pour it into a cooking pot.

Add in the correct proportion of sugar (or honey). Simmer over low heat for 10 minutes until the sugar is dissolved. Then bring to a rolling boil for 5 minutes. To test for doneness place a small amount of jelly on a cold plate (that has been prepared in the freezer) and put it in the freezer for 1 minute. If the jelly wrinkles when you push it with your finger, it's done. Take 1 tablespoon of the jam 3 to 5 times a day for diarrhea in adults and children.

CAUTION: Never eat Rowan berries raw. Women who are pregnant or breastfeeding should avoid them entirely. Overuse can cause stomach irritation, vomiting, diarrhea, and kidney damage.

Rowan Trees at Samhain

Make a necklace of the berries and equal-armed solar crosses of the wood bound with red thread. Place the crosses around the house and barn and hide them in your clothing. Have some Rowan berry jam for breakfast.

Saint John's Wort
(*Hypericum perforatum*)

Saint John's Wort is known to repel bad energies and offer magical protection; the mere scent of this plant is said to drive evil spirits away. The Welsh call it "The leaf of the blessed." In Brittany, the herb is still gathered in the old Druidic fashion—a person wearing loose, flowing clothing prays to the plant, asks its permission, and then picks it with their left hand, after carefully loosening the soil around the plant so the whole thing comes up at once.

For exorcisms, make a tea of Saint John's Wort and sea salt. Sprinkle the tea on every entrance and dark corner of the house and barn, then tie bags of Saint John's Wort to all the doorknobs.

Make equal-armed solar crosses of Rowan twigs or Elder branches, bound with red thread, and tie a red cloth sack of Saint John's Wort to each cross. Place these crosses on the front and back door. Sprinkle the crosses with blessed water every dark moon.

Before any ritual, drink Saint John's Wort tea with mint and honey to protect yourself.

Saint John's Wort oil is a classic preparation. *To make the oil:* Place fresh Saint John's Wort flowering tops and the uppermost leaves in a jar, barely cover them with oil, and leave them out in the sun until the oil turns blood red. This normally takes 1 to 2 weeks and can also be done in a hot, sunny window. Strain the oil and store in a cool, dark place. Anoint yourself with it in rituals as a protection, or add it to healing salves.

This plant has a great affinity for the nerves and is an excellent herb to poultice nerve injuries. Place a poultice of the leaves and flowers in the armpits to relieve nervous conditions and terrors.

Use the herb in salves with Germander (*Teucrium chamaedrys*) and Goldenrod (*Solidago* spp.) to treat wounds, burns, bruising, and skin problems.

A tea of the herb can be used as a wash to staunch bleeding.

Taken internally, Saint John's Wort tea calms bladder hysteria, bedwetting, insomnia, and cramps and other menstrual disorders. The flower tea is also useful for mild depression, nervous afflictions, anemia, headache, jaundice, and chest congestion.[24] Though known for its uplifting qualities, this herb is not a cure for clinical depression.

> **CAUTION: Saint John's Wort should not be taken internally for prolonged periods during the light half of the year because extended use leads to phototoxicity (I have personally witnessed this). Use it only in winter and stop taking it at least a month before you are likely to expose yourself to the sun. Avoid it if you are pregnant or breastfeeding or if you have Alzheimer's, ADHD, or bipolar disorder. This herb may cause mania in persons with major depression and may worsen schizophrenia. It may also worsen infertility issues and should be avoided before surgery. Children should not take it for more than 8 weeks.**

Saint John's Wort blooms at the time of the longest days, when summer is at its height. I like to make a Saint John's Wort liqueur at midsummer that is ready to drink at the winter solstice, bringing the warmth and light of our own nearest star into the darkest season.

🍃 Saint John's Wort Liqueur

> 2 cups water
> 2 cups organic sugar (or 1 cup raw, local honey)
> 2 cups Saint John's Wort flowers
> 2 cups chopped organic oranges, with the peel
> 2 cups vodka

Combine the water and sugar in a pan and warm over low heat. Stir until the sugar or honey is dissolved. Pour the sweetened water into a large glass jar. Add the flowers, oranges, and vodka. Cap tightly and store in a dark cupboard. Let steep for at least 6 months, shaking from time to time. Strain through cheese cloth until clear and serve.

Saint John's Wort at Samhain

In preparation for the season of Samhain, put bunches of Saint John's Wort into red cloth bags and hang them around the house and barn to repel evil spirits.

Make a solar cross of Rowan, Oak, or Elder, bound with red thread. Tie a red cloth bag of Saint John's Wort to the cross and hang it near the door.

Willow Tree
(*Salix* spp.)

Willow is one of the nine sacred woods suitable for the ritual fire at the Celtic fire festivals of Samhain, Imbolc, Beltaine, and Lughnasad. (The other sacred woods are Hazel, Alder, Birch, Ash, Yew, Elm, and Oak. The ninth wood can be Apple or Pine, or the ritual fire may be made entirely with Oak.)

To understand the sacredness of Willow we must look to the poets. In ancient Ireland, bardic harps were made of Willow wood, and poets would sit inside the "little cage" made by a drooping Willow tree to incubate a poem. Willow is a goddess tree; it acts as a guardian that protects from evil influence, and it is often planted near graves.

> For two centuries after the invasion of Henry II the voice of the muse was but feebly heard in Ireland. The bards fell with their country, and like the captive Israelites hung their untuned harps on the willows.[25]

Medicinally, Willow bark is valued for its ability to relieve pain, lower fever, and aid sleep. It is worth remembering that aspirin is actually a synthetic form of compounds found in Willow bark! You can use a tea of willow bark to ease the pains of rheumatism, arthritis, headache, muscle aches, and toothaches. ***To make the tea:*** Collect the inner bark of Willow in the spring (from a branch, never the trunk). Prepare it as a decoction (see page 7), or leave it to soak in cold water for 8 hours. Strain and drink.

> **CAUTION:** Avoid Willow bark during pregnancy and breastfeeding, if you are allergic or sensitive to aspirin, or if you have weak kidneys or a bleeding disorder. Long-term use (more than 12 weeks without a break) could damage the kidneys. Do not give Willow bark preparations to children with a fever or there is a danger of Reye's syndrome. Like aspirin, it could slow blood clotting, so avoid it before surgery.

Willow Tree at Samhain

Sit under a Willow and compose a poem in praise of the gods. Sing it at your Samhain rite. Add Willow wood to your ritual fire.

Woody Nightshade
(*Solanum dulcamara*)

Other common names for this herb include Snake Berry, Witch Flower, and Poison Berry, which should give you a hint about its nature.

Woody Nightshade was an ingredient in the "flying ointments" used by Witches. Were the Witches actually flying or just experiencing the sensation of flying?

Extracts of plants in the nightshade family were incorporated into a fatty base which was then rubbed on the body. Being fat-soluble, the tropane alkaloids were readily absorbed.

The earliest reference to the application of a flying ointment appears in a Latin novel of the first century, *The Golden Ass of Apuleius*. The hero, who is insatiably curious about magical practices, observes the witch Pamphile as she smears herself from head to toe with a salve and then flies away over the rooftops in the guise of an owl. (The modern Italian word for witch, *strega,* comes through the medieval *striga,* from the classical Latin *strix,* an owl.) As in the

Middle Ages, the power to fly was one of the chief attributes of the witch.[26]

Shepherds once protected themselves from the evil eye by wearing a necklace of Woody Nightshade berries. If they thought a cow or horse might fall victim to Witchcraft, they would put a garland of the berries around their neck too.

You can wear a spray of twigs, leaves, and berries pinned to your clothing to dispel the pain of unrequited love and hang it around the house and barn to protect yourself from evil sorcery. This must be done in secret.

Use Woody Nightshade in combination with Chamomile flowers (*Matricaria recutita*) in salves for swellings, bruises, and sprains. Use Woody Nightshade with Yellow Dock root (*Rumex crispus*) in salves for skin conditions and sores.

> **CAUTION: Take Woody Nightshade internally only under the supervision of an experienced herbalist. The stem tea has been used to increase secretions of the skin and kidneys, thus benefiting acne, scrofula, and ulcers, so it may be safe for internal use by adults when used with caution, but the berries and leaves are poisonous. Women who are pregnant or breastfeeding and children should avoid this plant. It can worsen irritable bowel syndrome.**

Woody Nightshade at Samhain

Make a necklace of Woody Nightshade berries and wear it for protection. Anoint yourself with a salve made from the twigs.

Yew
(*Taxus baccata, T. brevifolia, T. canadensis*)

Yew trees are associated with death and resurrection because when a mother Yew dies, she sends up shoots in a ring around herself, continuing to live on through her daughters. A Yew left undisturbed can live for thousands of years. One of the oldest trees in Europe is the Fortingall Yew in Perthshire, Scotland, said to be possibly five thousand years old.

In ancient Ireland, each province once had a sacred tree, and these were generally Ash or Yew.

Eó Mughna—Eó is the old Irish word for the Yew tree, yet legend claims the Eó Mughna was actually a mighty Oak. . . . It was supposedly located at Bealach Mughna, on the plain of Magh Ailbhe, now known as Ballaghmoon, Co Kildare.

Bile Tortan—Said to be an Ash, the Tree of Tortu stood at Ard Breccan, near Navan, Co Meath.

Eó Ruis—The Yew of Rossa was said to have stood at Old Leighlin, Co Carlow.

Craeb Daithí—The Branching Tree of Daithe was also a great Ash, located at Farbill, Co Westmeath.

Craeb Uisnig—This sacred tree, another Ash, was to be found at Uisneach, a hill which stood at the heart of what was once the High King's territory, known as Mide. It was considered the very centre point of Ireland.[27]

Yews are very common in English graveyards. The belief was that Yews would absorb bad odors and humors from decaying bodies; it was also said that sitting or sleeping near one could be fatal due to the "poisonous vapors" it might emit. In Brittany, it was held that a Yew planted in a graveyard would spread one root into the mouth of each corpse buried there.

Yews are used to decorate English churches at Whitson, a festival that can take place from mid-May to early June (the seventh Sunday after Easter). The observance incorporates aspects of the Pagan Beltaine celebration, with fairs, parades, Morris dancing, and women dressed in white. In the Scottish Highlands, Yew wood was said to ward off sorcerers and guard the milk. Yew can be burned to contact the spirits of the dead.

In a poem, Irish poet William Butler Yeats retells the ancient tale of Baile and Aillinn, which incorporates both Yews and Apples, trees with profound death associations. Apples are emblematic of Ynys Afallach, or Avalon, and Yew trees are symbolic of death, resurrection, and eternal life.

> ARGUMENT. Baile and Aillinn were lovers, but
> Aengus, the Master of Love, wishing them to be
> happy in his own land among the dead, told to each
> a story of the other's death, so that their hearts were
> broken and they died.

> . . . *And poets found, old writers say,*
> *A yew tree where his body lay;*
> *But a wild apple hid the grass*
> *With its sweet blossom where hers was,*
> *And being in good heart, because*
> *A better time had come again*
> *After the deaths of many men,*
> *And that long fighting at the ford,*
> *They wrote on tablets of thin board,*
> *Made of the apple and the yew,*
> *All the love stories that they knew.*
>
> FROM "BAILE AND AILLINN" (1903),
> BY W. B. YEATS

Yew trees have powerful effects on the body—so powerful, in fact, that they are generally poisonous. Yew trees have given us paclitaxel (Taxol), a drug used today to treat ovarian cancer. Homeopathic preparations of Yew can be safely taken for arthritis, gout, lung and bladder conditions, and pustular eruptions. A tea prepared from the needles can be used externally as a wash or fomentation for wounds.

CAUTION: Yew should be used only with expert supervision. Every part of this tree is poisonous except for the red flesh of the berries. Women who are pregnant or breastfeeding and children should avoid it entirely. The seeds found in the berries are poisonous too, but if they are swallowed and not chewed can be safely passed in a bowel movement.

Yew Tree at Samhain

Shave or rasp off a small pile of sawdust from a dry Yew branch and light it as you invoke your beloved dead.

⌒Herbs of Purification

The sacred energy of these herbs can be imparted to a room or a ritual area simply by hanging them in wreaths and sprays, burning them as incense, or even by putting them into a special dish on the coffee table. Bathing in a bath infused with these plants is also effective; your skin will absorb their energetic forces and colors. Many of these herbs are also culinary, so why not sneak them into your salads and other dishes as a type of kitchen witchery?

Basil (*Ocimum basilicum*)
Holy Basil, Tulsi (*Ocimum tenuiflorum*)

The name Basil is tied to that of the legendary basilisk, as noted in *A Modern Herbal* by Mrs. M. Grieve.

Some authorities say it comes from the Greek *basileus*, a king, because, as Parkinson [John Parkinson (1567–1650) was an English herbalist and one of the first notable English botanists] says, "the smell thereof is so excellent that it is fit for a king's house," or it may have been termed royal, because it was used in some regal unguent or medicine. One rather unlikely theory is that it is shortened from *basilisk*, a fabulous creature that could kill with a look. This theory may be based on a strange old superstition that connected the plant with scorpions. Parkinson tells us that "being gently handled it gave a pleasant smell but being hardly wrung and bruised would breed scorpions. It is also observed that scorpions doe much rest and abide under these pots and vessells wherein Basil is planted."[1]

Holy Basil (*Ocimum tenuiflorum*), or Tulsi, is a sacred plant in India, revered and even prayed to in the home because of its profound healing powers. The green-colored variety is called Lakshmi Tulsi and is sacred to the Hindu deity Lakshmi, goddess of love, wealth, and prosperity. The herb is prominent in ayurvedic medicine in which it is said to bring balance to the body, mind, and spirit. It is used for many conditions: as an anti-inflammatory, antioxidant, immune system modulator, and in treatments for conditions ranging from liver disease to arthritis, diabetes, and cancer.[2]

The purple-hued variety is called Krishna Tulsi. In Hindu belief, Tulsi, or Holy Basil, was the god Krishna's most beloved wife. Krishna Tulsi is used for fevers, coughs, colds, flu, sore throats, lung conditions, eye infections, migraines, heart problems, insect stings, and oral infections as well as to break up kidney stones and as a nerve tonic.[3]

Basil is known to purify, to drive unwanted ghosts or spirits from the house, to dispel grief, and to repel ill-intentioned sorcery. From Art of the Root (a New Age purveyor of herbal and magical products), we find instructions for a couple of Basil preparations.

Purification Spray: Simmer cut lemon and fresh basil in water. When cooled and added to a spray bottle, it can be used to clean sacred objects, candles, altars, spaces, the work environment, etc.

Exorcism Incense (to remove evil spirits from the home): Mix basil, rue, hyssop and myrrh and grind to a powder. Burn over a charcoal making sure you fumigated every corner of your home.[4]

As another protective measure, you can make a strong Basil tea and, after your usual bath or shower, use a cloth to wash every part of your body with the brew (do not rinse or towel it off, allow yourself to air-dry). Or add the Basil tea and sea salt to your daily bath. Do this for 9 days. Note: You can brew a large jar of strong Basil tea, cap it tightly, and keep it in the refrigerator. Use a small amount each day for 9 days.

Medicinally, Basil tea can be taken to relieve gas, colds, flu, headaches, constipation, kidney complaints, vomiting, and menstrual cramps. It can be gargled for sore throats. Basil can also be helpful in encouraging expulsion of the placenta after labor and to bring in breast milk.

CAUTION: Basil can be abortive, and medicinal doses should be avoided by women who are pregnant. Basil may worsen low blood sugar levels and may slow blood clotting. Stop use of this plant before surgery. Excessive use of the tea over long periods of time could harm the liver.

Use the herb externally to poultice wounds, scorpion stings, snake bites, insect bites, and acne.

Basil at Samhain

Make a strong Basil tea, put in some sea salt, and add it to your ritual bath before your Samhain ceremony. Also spray the tea around the ritual area before the participants arrive to repel any unwanted spirits.

Rue
(Ruta graveolens)

Sacred to Mars, Hecate, Diana, and Aradia, Rue is used to consecrate magical tools made of iron. It is useful for both purification and protection.

Rue is said to strengthen eyesight and also the "second sight." It removes hexes, curses, and unwanted spirits from the home and repels the evil eye and ill-intentioned Witchcraft. It sends bad magic back to the sender. Italians once wore tin or silver *cimaruta*—charms fashioned to look like Rue—as a form of protection. Today, you might hang bunches of rue in cloth bags on gateposts and doorknobs or place a large sprig over the door as protection from malefic ghosts and spirits.

Rue is commonly used in purification and protection baths; you can add a strong tea of Rue to the bathwater, or you might steep a bag of rue and sea salt in the tub while bathing. After the bath is finished, bury the bag of Rue in the ground.

Medicinally, warm Rue tea helps bring on menstruation. It is also useful for coughs, cramps, colic, upset stomach, diarrhea, heart palpitations, pleurisy, muscle spasms, nervous conditions, epilepsy, multiple sclerosis, Bell's palsy, hepatitis, and intestinal worms. Take no more than ½ cup per day. Use the tea as a gargle for sore throats, colds, and flu.

CAUTION: Large amounts of Rue can cause insomnia, dizziness, kidney and liver damage, and even death. Women who are pregnant or breastfeeding should avoid it. It could worsen gastrointestinal problems and irritate the urinary tract.[5]

Externally, Rue is anti-inflammatory and can be applied as a poultice or added to salves for sciatica, gout, rheumatic pain, bone injuries, dislocations and sprains, tumors, and warts. It can be used in a hot fomentation on the chest for bronchitis. The juice of the plant can be dripped into the ears to relieve earache.

A tiny amount of the fresh herb—try adding it to salads—can help improve eyesight, as can applications of the fresh juice directly to the eyes.

Pliny the Elder said of it:

It is good more particularly in cases of poisoning by wolf's bane and mistletoe, as well as by fungi, whether administered in the drink or the food. Employed in a similar manner, it is good for the stings of serpents; so much so, in fact, that weasels, when about to attack them, take the precaution first of protecting themselves by eating rue. Rue is good, too, for the injuries by scorpions and spiders, the stings of bees, hornets, and wasps, the noxious effects produced by cantharides and salamanders, and the bites of mad dogs.[6]

Rue at Samhain

Sprinkle Rue tea around the house or ritual circle, and use a branch of Rue to asperge the ritual site. Combined with other protective and purifying herbs (like Rosemary, Basil, Lavender, Mint, Sage, Vervain, and Yarrow, for example) in a bath or spray, it clears away negativity.

Sage
(*Salvia officinalis*)

I had a memorable experience with Sage when I moved into a new house years ago. A student had been recently struck and killed by a car while walking home, right in front of the house, and I was assigned her bedroom. Before moving in, I purified the room with burning Sage, making sure to fumigate the dark closet as well. When I did that, a huge white moth came fluttering out. I had cracked the window so that any ghoulies and ghosties could easily move on—the moth immediately found the open window and flew out. Almost instantly a blue jay caught the flying moth and ate it. The cycle was complete, and the moth was dead. I had a strong sense that the moth was the spirit of that recently deceased student.

White Sage (*Salvia apiana*) is a well-known Native American smudging herb; the scent of the smoke purifies an area of negative emotions and evil spirits. European Cunning Men and Cunning Women used Common or Garden Sage (*Salvia officinalis*) for the same reasons. Sage helps us deal with old grief, and it is said that those who eat Sage become immortal in wisdom and in years. Sage is sacred to Zeus and to Jupiter.

As noted on Witchipedia: The Online Encyclopedia of Magick, Folklore, and the Occult:

Sage is used in magical workings for immortality, longevity, wisdom, protection and the granting of wishes.

Sage is also believed to help alleviate sorrow of the death of a loved one.

To make a wish, write your wish on a sage leaf and sleep with it under your pillow for three days and then bury it.

Add sage to mojo bags to promote wisdom and to overcome grief.

Burn sage at funeral and remembrance ceremonies to help relieve the grief of the mourners.[7]

If you rub two leaves of Sage together, you will notice how dry they are. In herbal medicine, Sage is used to dry wet conditions. The leaf tea can help dry a wet cough, breast milk, perspiration, excessive saliva, night sweats, and diarrhea. Use the tea as a sore throat gargle and as a rinse for gum disease.

Sage can also help with painful menstruation and hot flashes as well as depression and memory loss.

Externally, apply Sage tea as a wash to cold sores and inhale the dried powdered leaves as a snuff for inflamed nasal passages.

Taking the tea 3 times daily for 2 months has been found to lower LDL ("bad cholesterol") levels in the blood.[8]

CAUTION: Do not take Sage for more than 4 months as the thujone it contains could cause liver or nervous system damage. Women who are pregnant should avoid the tea as it could cause miscarriage. Avoid when breastfeeding as it could stop the flow of milk. Diabetics should exercise caution with this plant as it can lower blood sugar levels. Monitor blood pressure too, because depending on the variety, Sage can lower or raise blood pressure. High amounts could trigger seizures in those who are prone to them. Stop taking Sage 2 weeks before surgery.[9]

🌱 Sage and Onion Dumplings*

Makes about 14 dumplings.

> 1½ tablespoons chopped fresh organic sage
> 2 large organic onions, chopped
> 4 cups breadcrumbs
> Sea salt and freshly ground organic white pepper
> 1 free-range, organic egg

*Adapted from Pamela Michael, *A Country Harvest* (New York: Exeter Books, 1987), 171.

2 tablespoons butter, melted

Fat or oil, for frying

Combine the sage, onions, breadcrumbs, and salt and pepper to taste in a large bowl. Mix well.

In a separate bowl, beat the egg with the melted butter. Add to the breadcrumb mixture and mix well. Separate the mixture into 14 even sections and, with floured hands, roll each section into a ball.

Set a large pan over medium-high heat and add enough fat or oil to fill it an inch or so. Drop the dumplings into the hot fat and fry for about 10 minutes on each side.

Sage at Samhain

Burn Sage in preparation for the Samhain rite. Smudge the ritual area, all magical tools, and all participants with the smoke as they enter the space.

Vervain
(Verbena hastata, V. officinalis)

The Eldrum Tree, a wonderful blog coming to us from the UK with lots of great folklore and history about traditional Celtic and European herbs, tells us this about Vervain:

The name "vervain" comes from the Celtic word "ferfaen," "fer" meaning to drive away and "faen" meaning a stone. Some authors believe that this describes the plant's ability to dissolve urinary calculi. The herb was beloved of the druids, being a main ingredient in their lustral [purificatory] water, as well as being used in the casting of spells and rituals, and for divinatory purposes. Vervain was used by the Romans as a ritual cleansing plant, and was made into brooms to sweep the altars. It was so beloved by the Romans that it had its own festival day of Verbenalia. It was used in love potions by Roman women. Interestingly, the plant could be used to both cast spells and ward a person against spells cast on them.

Traditionally, the plant was picked at the rising of the Dog Star

Sirius, at the dark of the moon just before flowering. It should be cut with a sacred sickle and lifted in the left hand, and gifts of honey should be given to the earth in recompense for the loss of the plant.[10]

A broom of Vervain's flowering tops is traditionally used in ritual to sweep and cleanse altars. Pliny the Elder notes:

With this the table of Jupiter is swept, and homes are cleansed and purified. There are two kinds of it; one has many leaves and is thought to be female, the other, the male, has fewer leaves. . . . Some authorities do not distinguish these two kinds but make of them one only, since both have the same properties. Both kinds are used by the people of Gaul in fortune-telling and in uttering prophecies, but the Magi especially make the maddest statements about the plant: that people who have been rubbed with it obtain their wishes, banish fevers, win friends, and cure all diseases without exception. . . . They say too that if a dining-couch is sprinkled with water in which this plant has been soaked the entertainment becomes merrier.[11]

Vervain is cleansing to almost every organ system in the body. A tea of Blue Vervain leaf (*Verbena hastata*) is taken for fever, dysentery, and diarrhea, including the acute diarrhea, especially in children, that often happens in summer. I suggest mixing Vervain with other more palatable herbs in tea, as it is quite bitter.

The aerial portions of Vervain have been used for asthma, whooping cough, angina and heart-centered edema, gout, gallbladder pain, anemia, digestive disorders, jaundice, and kidney and urinary tract problems. It can also benefit menopausal symptoms, irregular menstruation, and scanty milk production.

The root tea is used for stomach conditions such as gastroenteritis, viral or bacterial infection, and stomach flu and for cloudy urine.

Apply the leaf as a poultice to wounds, abscesses, burns, joint pains, and itching. The leaf tea makes a gargle for mouth and throat sores and for colds.[12]

CAUTION: Vervain is very bitter and could cause digestive upset or allergic reactions in some people. Women who are pregnant or breastfeeding should use it with discretion. Avoid the root entirely during pregnancy, as it may be abortive.

Important note: Some species, such as Narrow-Leafed Vervain, are now endangered due to habitat loss. Please be aware of the status of this plant in your area before you pick it!

Vervain at Samhain

Make a small broom of the plant to ritually sweep your altar. Make a tea and spray the chairs and table of your Dumb Supper before the guests arrive. Also, use it to spray the ritual area before your Samhain ceremony.

Yarrow
(Achillea millefolium)

Ayurvedic practitioner and medical herbalist Anne McIntyre notes:

The name yarrow is apparently derived from [the Greek word] *hieros,* which means sacred, because of the plant's association with ceremonial magic. Yarrow was thought to be richly endowed with spiritual properties, so it was preserved in temples and treated with special reverence. Its healing effect upon the blood was seen as an ability to influence the "life-blood," the essence or ego that is carried in the blood. It was used as an amulet, a charm to protect against negative energy and evil, capable of overcoming the forces of darkness and being a conductor of benevolent powers.[13]

The Yarrow

I WILL pluck the yarrow fair,
That more brave shall be my hand,
That more warm shall be my lips,
That more swift shall be my foot;

May I an island be at sea,
May I a rock be on land,
That I can afflict any man,
No man can afflict me.

TRADITIONAL SCOTTISH CHARM, AS DESCRIBED BY
ALEXANDER CARMICHAEL IN HIS NINETEENTH-
CENTURY *CARMINA GADELICA*

The Yarrow plant bears flowers of either white or pink. White Yarrow is better suited for general protection in stressful environments; it strengthens the aura and builds a shield of white light around you. Doctors, therapists, nurses, teachers who work with the emotionally unstable, and anyone who lives or labors in an environment with excess noise, fluorescent lights, industrial or traffic fumes, or positive ions emitted by office machinery and computers will benefit from this flower's purifying properties. Pink Yarrow is better suited to protection from strong emotional forces within yourself and coming from others. Pink Yarrow protects the heart and helps those who are overly sensitive to the feelings of other people.

Both types of Yarrow purify the mind and emotions by dispersing negative thoughtforms and psychic influences emanating from people and places.

You can strew white Yarrow across the threshold or hang wreaths and bags of white Yarrow on gateposts and doors to keep evil spirits from entering. You can also take Yarrow flower essence, 4 drops 4 times a day on the tongue, an hour before or after meals, or wash with it to increase your aura and strengthen your personal magical shields. (See pages 10–11 for instructions on making your own flower essences.)

For medicinal purposes, the parts used are the flowering tops and the leaf. Take Yarrow as a tea with honey for coughs, bronchitis, and headaches; the tea also benefits the liver, kidneys, and digestion and is helpful for diarrhea. Combine Yarrow with Peppermint (*Mentha piperita*) and Elderflower (*Sambucus* spp.) to make a tea for stomach flu. A few drops of the fresh juice, diluted in milk, juice, or water, can be given to a child with an upset stomach.

Use Yarrow tea externally as a wash for sore eyes (filter through an organic coffee filter before applying to the eyes) and as a wash for sores and ulcers. Use the herb as a styptic poultice for wounds and bleeding hemorrhoids, or combine mashed Yarrow and Chamomile flowers (*Matricaria recutita*) to poultice abscesses and tumors. Dry and powder the leaves to make a snuff for asthma and headaches.

> **CAUTION:** Yarrow may cause drowsiness and increased urination in some. Women who are pregnant or breastfeeding should avoid it. It may slow blood clotting, so avoid it before surgery. It may cause allergic response in those who are sensitive to the Aster family of plants (Ragweed, Chrysanthemum, Marigold, Daisy, etc.).[14]

How to Cook with Yarrow*

Yarrow is an edible and nutritious herb. Gather the small, fresh leaves in early spring and add them to your salads. The very young spring leaves of Yarrow taste best, but in the fall you can still pick leaves from the top of the plant. Kitchen Witches will appreciate the many ways magical Yarrow can be incorporated into a meal!

Yarrow leaves can be used as a substitute for Tarragon, and you can mix them with Parsley, Chervil, and Tarragon as a flavoring agent. Sprinkle Yarrow on meats and vegetables at the end of cooking, to preserve flavor, the way you would add fresh chopped Parsley to a dish (heating the leaves too much ruins the taste).

Use Yarrow in marinades and vinaigrettes and mix it with Parsley to make a flavored oil. *To make the oil:* Combine ½ cup Parsley, ½ cup flavorless oil (such as olive oil), and ¼ cup Yarrow; puree in a blender and let steep for a few days, strain and bottle.

Try adding chopped Yarrow, Parsley, and Garlic to pasta dishes. Sprinkle a tiny amount on fresh fruit and yogurt. It can even be added to sorbet and ice cream.

*Cooking tips for Yarrow adapted from Allen Bergo's "Cooking with Yarrow?" Forager Chef (website).

Yarrow at Samhain

Make bags or wreaths of Yarrow and hang them on doors and gateposts as protection. Drink a tiny bit of the Yarrow flower essence to strengthen your personal shields and purify your mind and emotions in preparation for the approaching winter.

Visionary Herbs and Herbs of Divination

When using these plants, it will be especially important to ground, center, and pay close attention to any cautions, especially if you are taking any medications, ***whether they are over-the-counter or prescribed.*** Please take the time to do your research; before beginning to use any of the herbs, find out whether they have interactions with your medications or whether they are contraindicated for you given your particular health profile.

As always, call upon your own protective deities and spirits to guide you in this work.

Apple Tree
(*Malus* spp.)

For more on the lore, history, and usage of Apple, see page 16.

I have a large, flat, shamanic drum on which I have painted the letters of the Ogham (the ancient Irish pre-Christian alphabet). To divine answers to questions I hold the drum flat and place a bunch of Apple seeds in a circle in the center of the drum. I play the drum gently with a leather covered beater until one of the seeds pops onto a letter, giving me a divinatory clue.

Apples at Samhain

Just before midnight on Samhain, cut an Apple into nine sections and carry the pieces to a dark room with a mirror. At the stroke of midnight begin eating the Apple pieces while staring into the mirror. When you get to the ninth section, throw it behind you and the face of your future lover should appear.

Alternatively, at midnight on Samhain, throw freshly peeled Apple parings over your shoulder and see what letter they form to divine the initials of your next lover.

If you have more than one potential future lover, press apple seeds to your cheek and name each seed for a potential mate. The last seed to stick to you will be your true love.

Cannabis
(Cannabis sativa, C. indica, C. ruderalis)

Cannabis is slowly becoming legalized in the United States. Besides being a wonderful medicinal for anxiety, PTSD, depression, chronic pain, and other disorders, Cannabis enables the user to slow down and be more "in the moment" during a ritual, especially a rite involving trance dancing, guided meditation, or other visualizations.

Cannabis was used in ancient funerals to honor the dead. The ancient Scythians were among those who incorporated Cannabis into their funerary rites.

> After the death and burial of their king, the Scythians would purify themselves by setting up small tepee-like structures which they would enter to inhale the fumes of hemp seeds (and the resinous flower calyxes surrounding the seeds) thrown onto red-hot stones.
>
> In a famous passage written in about 450 B.C., Herodotus describes these funeral rites as follows: ". . . when, therefore, the Scythians have taken some seed of this hemp, they creep under the cloths and put the seeds on the red-hot stones; but this being put on smokes, and produces such a steam, that no Grecian vapour-bath would surpass it. The Scythians, transported by the vapour, shout aloud."[1]

During the Hindu festival of Holi, people drink *bhang*, which is made from Cannabis flowers. According to the Hindu tradition, long ago the *devas* (gods) and *asuras* (demons) joined forces to churn the seas to create *amrita* (the elixir of life) to guarantee their own immortality. The god Shiva created Cannabis from his own body to purify the elixir. When a drop of that elixir fell to Earth, the Cannabis plant was born. Now people drink bhang to unite with Shiva and to have a fortunate reincarnation.

Mexican devotees of Santa Muerte (Saint of Death, Holy Death) purify themselves with Cannabis smoke and use it as incense in their rituals, perhaps as an agent to more easily contact the saint. As a personification of death, Santa Muerte is associated with healing, protection, and safe delivery to the afterlife. She is a continuation of the Aztec goddess of death Mictecacihuatl, or Mictlancihuatl (Nahuatl for "Lady of the Dead").

Magu (the Hemp Maiden) is a Taoist goddess of the elixir of life and protector of females. Her name derives from *ma* (Cannabis) and *gu* (aunt or maid). She is the creatress, progenitress, and great goddess of creation myths associated with long life, rebirth, and good fortune. *Cannabis sativa* grows on Mount Tai, the mountain sacred to this goddess, and Taoists once burned Cannabis in their ritual censers to induce visions and more easily communicate with the dead.

Cannabis has been used medicinally in cultures across the world for millennia, from Egypt and Mesopotamia to Africa, India, China, Japan, and beyond. It is taken as a tea or tincture for spasmodic asthma, chronic spasmodic cough, fever with delirium and wakefulness, endometriosis with spasms, anorexia nervosa or loss of appetite due to a long illness, colitis, hemorrhoids, rectal prolapse, insomnia with nightmares, cystitis and urethritis (especially when there is irritability), gout, pruritus with itching, neuropathy, and spasmodic conditions associated with depression. It has an excellent reputation for its use in pain management, whether as a tea, tincture, or poultice.

The leaves (fresh or frozen) can be taken in a smoothie as an immune enhancer; they will not get you high.

Cannabis can be smoked to ease the eye pressure of glaucoma.

CAUTION: Chronic usage of Cannabis may cause amotivational syndrome (aimlessness and poor communication). Withdrawal symptoms may include anorexia, insomnia, anxiety, and depression. Smoking it during pregnancy could result in miscarriage or an underweight fetus. Cannabis may also cause dysphoria, tachycardia, and orthostatic hypotension and may abruptly cause the manifestation of latent schizophrenia.

Note: To avoid these problems, many people are now using CBD oil, an extract derived from Cannabis with high levels of cannabidiol, a constituent thought to have profound healing effects without the psychoactive effects. People are also turning to Cannabis strains with minimal THC (tetrahydrocannabinol), the compound that triggers the psychoactive effects.

🌿 How to Make a Cannabis Salve*

Different strains of Cannabis are used for different conditions. For example, high-CBD/low-THC strains are used for epilepsy, intense anxiety, inflammation, and fatigue. Strains with roughly equal amounts of CBD and THC are good for pain, mild anxiety, insomnia, and inflammation. For a topical salve that is suited to the pains of ordinary life, I suggest a high-CBD/low-THC variety. Get your buds from a reputable dispensary, of course.

Part One: Create CBD-Infused Oil

To make the oil, bake Cannabis buds in a 230°F oven for about 40 minutes, then transfer them to a glass or ceramic jar. This heating makes the Cannabis compounds more bioavailable. Add just enough oil (coconut oil, almond oil, olive oil, or a mixture of these) to barely cover the buds. Cap the jar. Let the buds infuse in the oil for about a week. Every few days, warm the jar in a hot water bath and shake well to evenly distribute the leaves and oil. Strain out the buds, and then repeat the process with fresh buds, using the same oil. The twice-infused will have a high CBD content.

---

*Adapted from Colleen Codekas's "How to Make Cannabis CBD Infused Oil" and "How to Make Cannabis CBD Salve," *Grow Forage Cook Ferment* (blog).

You can also make a separate cold infusion and when it is done, combine it with your warmed infusion. Use a 1 to 5 ratio of plant to oil, let it steep 2 to 4 weeks, shaking every few days. Warm infusions and cold infusions will extract slightly different plant constituents.

Part Two: Create the Salve

> 1 cup CBD-infused oil (as made above or purchased)
> 1 ounce beeswax, grated or cut into small chunks*
> 1 ounce shea butter

Combine the CBD-infused oil and beeswax in a double boiler or bain-marie. Heat gently and stir continuously until the wax melts. Add the shea butter and stir well. Pour the mixture into very clean jars or tins.

Allow the salve to cool and harden for a few hours before you cap the jars. Put on the lids and store in a cool, dark place.

---

*A very easy way to break up beeswax is to place it in the freezer in a paper or plastic bag. When it is completely frozen, take it out and simply hit it with a hammer. It will shatter into small pieces.

Cannabis at Samhain

If it's legal in your state, why not pass around a bowl? Add Cannabis to a ritual incense mix. Anoint your third eye, temples, heart, and hands with Cannabis salve before your Samhain rite to honor the dead.

Hazel
(Corylus avellana)

Hazel is a tree of wisdom, inspiration, and poetry, and its nuts are eaten before divination. Hazelnuts are a goddess herb because of the milk of the green nut. Other plants with milky saps are assigned to goddesses, for example the milky latex that is found in dandelion stems marks this plant as sacred to Irish goddess Brighid.

Hazelnuts are both nutritious and healing. The ancient Celts mixed chopped Hazelnuts with their porridge as a strengthening food. Hazel nuts can also be ground and mixed with mead and honey to make a drink for chronic coughs. Add a pinch of Cayenne Pepper to help discharge phlegm.

Hazelnuts at Samhain

On Samhain Eve, place Hazelnuts in the fire, after assigning a name to each nut. The first nut to pop out of the flames reveals the name of your future spouse.

See page 134 for more on Hazelnuts and their use as a ritual offering for Samhain celebrations.

Mugwort
(*Artemisia vulgaris*)

Mugwort is a classic herb for "dream pillows" because it opens the third eye. It is an excellent herb for those who are attempting astral travel and vision, and it enhances visions for those pursuing lucid dreaming.

Here is a bit of my own experience with this herb: Years ago, I created a "dream tea" that was doled out during an evening ritual at a large Pagan festival. It contained mostly Mugwort with small amounts of Yarrow (for protection), Rose petals (for love and sweetness), and honey. I drank two large cups of the brew and walked out into the night. It was the full moon, and I was easily able to navigate my way through the camp to the edge of a lake. I sat down and half closed my eyes, preparing to meditate beside the waters. I suddenly realized that I could see to the bottom of the lake; the plants down there were glowing with many colors and waving gently from the depths. That vision persisted for a few minutes and then gradually faded.

The Ainu of Japan burn Mugwort to exorcise the spirits of disease, who are said to flee from the smell. In China, people hang bunches of Mugwort during the annual Dragon Boat Festival to keep away both bugs and evil spirits.

From pre-Christian Pagan times to the present, Mugwort has been one of the most important herbs for healing and divination. In 1927 Germany it was still being used to treat sickness caused by sorcery and to undo bewitchment of eggs and milk. Modern Witches make Dream Pillows—pillows stuffed with Mugwort leaves and possibly some Lavender flowers or Heather blossoms for added relaxation—to sleep on and drink Mugwort tea to enhance dreaming and to open the third eye, the *ajna chakra,* which is located in the center of the brow, above the nose. Once awakened the third eye allows one to see the inner and outer worlds more clearly and to understand the world from the point of mindful witness or observer.

Wear a crown or belt of Mugwort as protection during a rite to summon spirits. Hang bunches of Mugwort on gateposts and over the door to keep evil spirits out of the house. Make a strong tea (or use the oil) to cleanse and bless magical tools.

Grow Mugwort near the house and commune with it regularly to open your psychic powers. Hang bunches of Mugwort near your bed or stuff it into a pillow to promote visionary dreams and to contact the ancestors. Drink Mugwort tea and burn the leaves or smoke them at a funeral to communicate with the deceased. Burn Mugwort near a grave to protect the spirit of the deceased and to release their sadness (especially if the death was traumatic in some way).

Mugwort is part of the famous Saxon "Nine Herbs Charm" (see box on pages 32–33).

> *Remember, Mugwort, what you made known,*
> *What you arranged at the great proclamation.*
> *You were called Una, the oldest of herbs,*
> *you have power against three and against thirty,*
> *you have power against poison and against infection,*
> *you have power against the loathsome foe roving*
>   *through the land.*
>
> From the tenth-century Old English
> "Nine Herbs Charm"

In addition to its visionary and divinatory uses, Mugwort has long been used for its medicinal effects. Taken as a tea, it helps with issues in the digestive tract such as diarrhea, cramps, constipation, and vomiting. It is a classic herb for premenopausal syndrome (PMS) and irregular periods. Thanks to its sedative properties, it can aid with anxiety, epilepsy, convulsions in children, chronic fatigue and depression (neurasthenia), preoccupation with illness (hypochondria), general irritability, restlessness, and insomnia. It is a tonic for the liver.

Mugwort can also be added to healing salves and appears to be especially well suited for itchy skin conditions such as burn scars.

> **CAUTION: Women who are pregnant or breastfeeding should avoid Mugwort. It may cause allergic hypersensitivity, especially in those who are allergic to Chamomile, Birch, Celery, Wild Carrot, and other members of the Aster family, as well as those who are allergic to Tobacco, White Mustard, honey, royal jelly, Hazelnut, Olive, latex, Peach, Kiwi, the Micronesian nut called Nangai, and other plants from the genus _Artemisia_, including Sage.[2]**

Mugwort at Samhain

Visit the grave of a wise beloved ancestor, or of any deceased person whose advice you need. Bring a thermos of hot Mugwort tea and drink it at their graveside. Burn Mugwort and inhale the smoke near the grave. After you have heard the voice of your beloved dead or seen their image, give them a gift such as a flower, a lit candle in a jar, and some small coins, and you may leave with a tiny bit of soil for your magical workings.

Think carefully about which deceased person you will collect soil from. If you want to do healing work, find the grave of a healer or a physician. If you want to climb a mountain, find the grave of a successful mountaineer. If you want to make art, seek out the grave of a famous artist, and so on, and always leave them a gift and a few coins so you can "buy the dirt."

Tobacco
(_Nicotiana_ spp.)

Believe it or not, Tobacco is classified as a hallucinogen, and for those of us who have never developed the Tobacco habit, it certainly acts like one. In many Native American cultures, it is a sacred plant whose leaves are offered to elders as a sign of respect. When smoked or placed on the ground or upon water with reverence, Tobacco attracts spirits so we can commune with them, and it also sends our prayers of thanks to the Earth and heavens.

Burn Tobacco in your ritual space when you petition the dead. Smudge a person, place, or thing with Tobacco (or Sage) smoke to break a curse, following up by smudging with sweet herbs like Copal (*Hymenaea courbaril, Hymenaea verrucosa, Shorea javanica*), Holy Wood (a.k.a. Palo Santo, *Bursera graveolens*), and Sweet Grass (*Hierochloe odorata*) to draw in peaceful and positive energies.

When a nasty storm approaches the house, place Tobacco on the ground in the four directions as protection. Offer Tobacco to the land spirits when you gather plants or stones for food or healing work. This kind of thanks offering has been given for thousands of years here in America, and the land spirits understand it.

In the New Orleans Voodoo tradition, Tobacco is offered at a crossroads to communicate with the spirits of the dead, and it is buried at the four corners of a property to protect the home. Tobacco is also burned in an herbal mix to purify the home of unwanted spirits.

Tobacco is a sacred ritual herb of *santeros,* the practitioners of Santería, an Afro-Cuban religion that is a blend of African beliefs and Catholicism. A modern Cuban Witch named Mayra uses Tobacco cigars in ceremony to induce a trance, resulting in spontaneous shaking and words of divination from the spirits as reported by the following observer.

One day I was at Mayra's place and Dayana, an 18-year-old Cuban model, showed up. Dayana was having some troubles at home so her mother decided to take her along to cleanse her of bad spirits, something known as a "rompimiento" ceremony.

The ritual consists of rites and prayers involving coconuts, cigar smoke, alcohol, scents and other artefacts. The person must have his or her clothes ripped off as part of the process to expel bad spirits.

The momentum of the ceremony kept growing; Mayra was smoking cigars, the room was full of smoke, and there was a strong smell of different scents as Mayra seemed to fall into a trance. At one point, in her dazed state, she had to be held up by her husband. She asked Dayana to follow her to the back of the house near her shrine, and started ripping off her clothes frantically while speaking in an African language.[3]

Tobacco is smoked in sacred pipes in many Native American traditions, the burning smoke lifts skyward the prayers of peace and blessing for all beings on Earth. One of the travesties of modern culture is the way we have abused sacred Tobacco by becoming habitually addicted to it. The result of such mindless overuse is often illness and death. If you are addicted to this herb, why not at least make a prayer each time you light up?

In pre-Columbian times, Tobacco had many medicinal uses in the New World.

> In 1529, a Spanish missionary priest, Bernadino de Sahagun, collected information from four Mexican physicians about use of tobacco for medicinal purposes. He recorded that breathing the odour of fresh green leaves of the plant relieved persistent headaches. For colds and catarrh, green or powdered leaves should be rubbed around inside the mouth. Diseases of glands in the neck could be cured by cutting out the root of the lesion and placing on it crushed tobacco plant hot and mixed with salt, on the same spot. . . . In 1934 Fernando Ocaranza summed up the medicinal uses of tobacco in Mexico before 1519 as antidiarrheal, narcotic and emollient; he said that tobacco leaves were applied for the relief of pain, used in powdered form for the relief of catarrh and applied locally to heal wounds and burns.[4]

When placed on bleeding wounds, Tobacco will staunch the flow of blood and relieve pain—I saw this for myself years ago when I was privileged to attend a Sun Dance ritual. If you have Tobacco in the house and you happen to cut yourself in the kitchen, try applying the crushed leaf to your injury as a styptic.

Tobacco at Samhain

Add a pinch of organic Tobacco leaf to your incense mix to purify the home and ritual space. Burn a bit of Tobacco as you contact the ancestors.

Plate 26 (left). Lichens

Plate 27 (right). Lotus
(*Nelumbo nucifera*)

Plate 28. Maidenhair Spleenwort
(*Asplenium trichomanes*)

Plate 29. Mandrake (*Mandragora officinarum, M. autumnalis*)

Plate 30. Marjoram (*Origanum majorana*)

Plates 31 (left) and 32 (right). Marsh Mallow (*Althaea officinalis*)

Plate 33 (left). Mistletoe (*Viscum album*)

Plates 34 (top right) and 35 (bottom). Mugwort (*Artemisia vulgaris*)

Plates 36 (left) and 37 (right).
Mullein (*Verbascum thapsus*)

Plate 38. Myrrh
(*Commiphora myrrha*)

Plate 39 (left). Nettles
(*Urtica* spp.)

Plate 40 (right) Oak Tree
(*Quercus* spp.)

Plate 41. Oak Tree
(English variety, *Quercus pedunculata*)

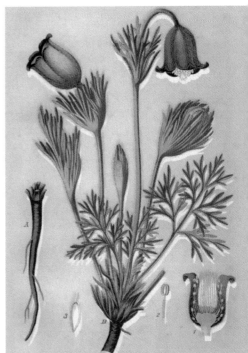

Plate 42 (left). Parsley
(*Petroselinum crispum*)

Plate 43 (right).
Pasqueflower, Pulsatilla
(*Anemone pulsatilla*)

Pulegium vulgare. Mill.
Polei.

Plate 44. Pennyroyal
(*Mentha pulegium*)

Plate 45. Periwinkle
(*Vinca minor, V. major*)

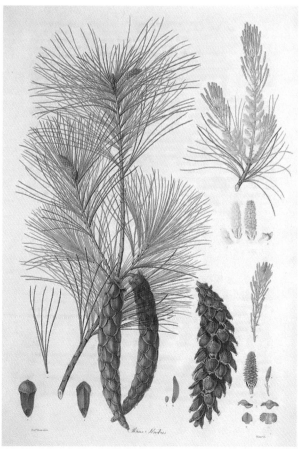

Plate 46. Pine
(*Pinus* spp.)

Plate 47. Pumpkin
(*Cucurbita pepo*)

Plate 48. Rosemary
(*Rosmarinus officinalis*)

ᴴᴇᴿᴮꜱ ᴛᴏ ᴄᴏᴍᴍᴜɴɪᴄᴀᴛᴇ WITH, ᴿᴇʟᴇᴀꜱᴇ, ᴀɴᴅ ᴴᴏɴᴏʀ ᴛʜᴇ ᴅᴇᴀᴅ

Many cultures recognize those times when the veil between the worlds is thin and celebrate with festivals to honor the dead, from the well-known Día de los Muertos (Day of the Dead) in Mexico to Fete Ghede in Haiti, the Hungry Ghost Festival in China, and the Bon Festival in Japan, and Pchum Ben in Cambodia, to name just a handful. In the ancient traditions of Celtic Europe, Samhain has long been celebrated as the ideal time to communicate with the beloved dead.

Our modern Western culture tends to be afraid of death; it is generally considered a taboo subject, and we do not speak about it socially or grieve publicly. We have no established rituals, other than funerals, for honoring loved ones who have died.

Nevertheless, the dead are, of course, all around us. They help us in unseen ways and make their presence known in both subtle and unsubtle ways. My aunt Jackie crossed the veil on the evening of the winter solstice. Aunt Jackie was very fond of birthdays and never forgot to send a card or a gift. Her best friend, Lucy, was with her when she passed over. Lucy had a birthday in December, and a week or so after Aunt Jackie passed, a strange message appeared on my answering machine. A distant, deep, breathy, ancient-sounding lady's voice said, "Don't forget her birthday."

Pay attention to those on the other side and keep track of your dreams about them. They surround you and are with you always. You are their voice and hands on this side of the veil. The herbs profiled in this chapter can help you stay in touch with, honor, and assist them.

Embalming Herbs

The ancient Egyptians used the following herbs and materials to preserve their dead: Myrrh (*Commiphora myrrha*), Sandalwood (*Santalum album*), attar of Rose (*Rosa* spp.), Cedar (especially Cedar of Lebanon, *Cedrus libani*), salt, Cinnamon (*Cinnamomum verum, C. cassia*), Frankincense (*Boswellia sacra*), Laudanum (tincture of opium, extracted from *Papaver somniferum*), Saffron (*Crocus sativus*), Orris root (*Iris* spp.), Storax (extracted from *Liquidambar orientalis*), and Gum Mastic (extracted from *Pistacia lentiscus* var. *chia*).

These herbs and substances would have been used in embalming mixtures and to wash body cavities. In modern times many people are hoping for a "green burial" that avoids the chemicals and poisons that are often used by the funeral industry. I suggest that these ancient herbs could be incorporated as oils or a dusting powder or wash for the corpse.

Aspen, Poplar Tree
(*Populus balsamifera, P. nigra, P. tremula, P.* spp.)

For lore, history, and usage of Aspen, see page 19. The trembling leaves of Aspen carry messages to the spirits. Sit beneath a Poplar and send your prayers to the wind.

Asphodel
(*Asphodelus ramosus*)

With its gray foliage, this is said to be a favorite food of the dead. In ancient Greece, the living roasted the roots and ate them, or dried and powdered the roots and added them to bread dough. Considered a delicacy, the cooked roots or bread were left as gifts on graves.

Asphodel was planted on graves in the Mediterranean area, where it is native, and was used to ritually bathe corpses. In fact, according to Greek mythology, Hades, the realm of the dead, had a special section called Asphodel Meadows where ghosts were said to reside. In his poem "Asphodel, That Greeny Flower," William Carlos Williams writes, "I was cheered / when I came first to know / that there were flowers also / in hell."

In the Odyssey, Homer writes:

> *down the dank*
> *mouldering paths and past the Ocean's streams they went*
> *and past the White Rock and the Sun's Western Gates*
> *   and past*
> *the Land of Dreams,*
> *and soon they reached the fields of asphodel*
> *where the dead, the burnt-out wraiths of mortals make*
> *   their home*
>
> HOMER, *ODYSSEY* 24.5–9,
> TRANSLATION BY ROBERT FAGLES

Asphodel also has medicinal uses. The root, gathered in the spring, is used to poultice swellings and infections. The root tea is antispasmodic, brings on menstruation, and contains colchicine, a compound that can help those with gout, but probably should be used internally with great caution, especially by those suffering from nephritis or gastritis.

CAUTION: Asphodel root is poisonous if taken in excessive quantities. Avoid this plant if you are pregnant or breastfeeding.

Asphodel at Samhain

If you live in an area where it grows, leave the flower (or plant one) on a grave.

Belladonna, Deadly Nightshade
(Atropa belladonna)

Atropa belladonna is named after Atropos, one of the Greek Fates who comes with her magical blade to cut the threads of life when a person is dying. This herb is very appropriate for funerals; add a few drops of the tincture to the water used to asperge the ritual area and the corpse to help the spirit let go and move on.

Herbalist Crystal Aneira tells us:

> It is an herb of the Underworld and connected with underworld deities. As such it may be used to consecrate tools used for underworld contacts, particularly those made of lead or onyx. It can be added to the Samhain incense, providing that it is used in the open air, to attract the Ancient Dead to the feast.[1]

Belladonna was a traditional ingredient in Witches' flying ointments. It is thought to have been combined with opium poppy and other poisonous plants, in which case, perhaps, the combination of "belladonna's tropane alkaloids and opiate alkaloids in the opium poppy causes a dream-like waking state . . . [that is sometimes] posited as the explanation of how flying ointments might have actually worked in contemporary writing on witchcraft."[2]

Francis Bacon, English philosopher and scientist of the late 1600s, lists the following ingredients for Witches' flying ointment.

> . . . the fat of children digged out of their graves, of Juices of small-age (wild celery), wolf-bane and cinquefoil, mingled with the meal of fine wheat . . . henbane, hemlock,* mandrake, moon-shade, or rather night-shade, tobacco, opium, saffron, poplar leaves (Balm of Gillead), &c.[3]

> *Here's monk's-hood, that breeds fever in the blood;*
> *And deadly nightshade, that makes men see ghosts;*

---

*By Hemlock he means Water Hemlock (*Cicuta virosa*), not the Hemlock tree.

And henbane, that will shake them with
convulsions . . .

FROM *GILES COREY OF THE SALEM FARMS* (1900),
BY HENRY WADSWORTH LONGFELLOW

Though Belladonna is widely known as a poisonous herb, its leaf and root have been used in medicinal preparations for spasmodic coughs and asthma, Parkinson's Disease, hay fever, and even colic. For external use, it is added to salves for rheumatism, sciatica, neuralgia, excessive sweating, and psychiatric hyperkinesis. It is also added to hemorrhoid suppositories.

CAUTION: Belladonna should not be used without expert supervision. Women who are pregnant or breastfeeding should avoid it. It can worsen congestive GI tract infections and blockages, stomach ulcers, hiatal hernia, high blood pressure, rapid heartbeat, heart failure, urinary retention, constipation, and esophageal reflux. It may cause a person with a fever to overheat. It can be harmful to those with Down's syndrome. It can worsen psychiatric disorders and cause hallucinations, convulsions, and coma.[4] In other words, don't try this at home!

To safely take advantage of Belladonna's healing powers while avoiding its poisonous nature, look to homeopathic formulations. William Boericke's *Homeopathic Materia Medica* (1927), a classic textbook in the field, tells us that the following symptoms and conditions would yield to Belladonna.

Hot, red skin, flushed face, glaring eyes, throbbing carotids, excited mental state, hyperesthesia of all senses, delirium, restless sleep, convulsive movements, dryness of mouth and throat with aversion to water, neuralgic pains that come and go suddenly (Oxytropis). Heat, redness, throbbing and burning. Epileptic spasms followed by nausea and vomiting. Scarlet fever and also prophylactic. Here use the thirtieth potency. Exophthalmic goitre. No thirst, anxiety or fear. Belladonna stands for [that is, its use is indicated by] violence of attack and suddenness of onset.[5]

Belladonna at Samhain

If you are performing your ritual outdoors (not if you're indoors!), burn a bit of Belladonna as an incense. Make a tea and use it to ritually clean your magical tools at the start of the Celtic New Year.

Black Fava Beans
(Vicia faba)

Black Fava Beans played a prominent role in funerary rites in ancient Rome. The beans were eaten at funerals and distributed to the poor on the anniversary of a death. At a funeral, a barefoot priest would appear carrying Black Fava Beans. After washing his hands, he would fling the beans over his shoulder and say nine times, "With these beans, I redeem myself and mine." The priest would avoid looking behind him because it was believed that the spirit of the departed stood behind him to gather up the beans.

The Romans believed that the souls of their ancestors resided inside Black Fava Beans because within each bean was a visible plant embryo. At weddings, the bride and groom consumed them in hopes of attracting the soul of a deceased ancestor to continue the family line.

🪔 Vitellian (Roman) Beans*

This recipe comes directly from a first-century collection of recipes from the era of the Roman Empire.

Vitellian peas or beans: Cook the peas or beans; when you have skimmed them, put in leek and coriander and mallow flowers. While it is cooking, pound pepper, lovage, oregano, fennel seed; pour on liquamen† and wine, put in the pan, add oil. When it is simmering, stir it, pour green oil on top and serve.

Decorate the dish with fresh mallow leaves and flowers and serve

---

*Adapted from C. Grocock and S. Grainger, *Apicius: A Critical Edition with an Introduction and English Translation* (London: Prospect Books, 2006).

†*Liquamen* or *garum* is a Roman fish sauce. You could substitute Vietnamese *nuoc mam* or Thai *nam pla*, which are made with fermented fish, salt, and water. But you can also make your own garum. Find a recipe online at the Coquinaria website.

with goat cheese, a round loaf of freshly baked bread, and a good Mediterranean wine.

Black Fava Beans at Samhain

Serve a soup made with the beans in honor of your ancestors.

Chervil
(Myrrhis odorata)

Chervil is said to facilitate communication with the dead. As an herb of immortality, it places us in touch with our own eternal selves and thus closer to the realm in which the beloved dead reside. Richard Folkard spoke of Witches' use of Chervil in his book *Plant Lore, Legends, and Lyrics,* published in 1884.

> The chief strength of poor witches lies in the gathering and boiling of herbs. . . . Chervil and Pennyroyal are used because they both have the effect of making anyone tasting their juices see double.[6]

Chervil was also an ingredient in the ancient Saxon's "Nine Herbs Charm" (see box on pages 32–33).

Chervil is a common garden herb used in cooking similarly to Parsley. Medicinally, the juice of the herb and root are taken for eczema (try a teaspoonful in water). A tea of the flowering herb can be used for coughs, gout, abscesses, anemia, digestive issues, and high blood pressure, while the root decoction makes an antiseptic wound wash. You can also use this plant in salves for wounds and gout.

CAUTION: Avoid medicinal doses of Chervil during pregnancy as it may cause genetic mutations in the fetus.

Chervil at Samhain

Add Chervil to the tea or liqueur in your ritual cup. Burn dried Chervil on your altar as you converse with the ancestors.

Dittany of Crete
(Origanum dictamnus)

This herb is sacred to Persephone and Osiris and is said to improve communication with the dead.

Aleister Crowley wrote of using dittany in a ceremony to summon the "Goetia demon Buer," said to be a president in Hell.

> The temple was approximately 16 feet by 8, and 12 high. A small "double-cube" altar of acacia was in the centre of a circle; outside this was a triangle in which it was proposed to get the demon to appear. The room was thick with the smoke of incense, some that of Abramelin,* but mostly, in a special censer in the triangle, Dittany of Crete (we decided to use this, as H.P.B. [Helena Petrovna Blavatsky] once said that its magical virtue was greater than that of any other herb).
>
> As the ceremony proceeded, we were aware that the smoke was not uniform in thickness throughout the room, but tended to be almost opaquely dense in some parts of it, all but clear in others. This effect was much more definite than could possibly be explained by draughts, or by our own movements. Presently it gathered itself together still more completely, until it was roughly as if a column of smoke were rising from the triangle, leaving the rest of the room practically clear.
>
> Finally, at the climax of the ritual—we had got as far as the "stronger and more potent conjuration"—we both saw, vaguely enough, but yet beyond doubt, parts of a quite definite figure.[7]

Madame Helena Blavatsky described the plant this way:

> Diktamnon (Gr.), or Dictemnus (Dittany). A curious plant possessing very occult and mystical properties and well-known from ancient times. It was sacred to the Moon-Goddesses Luna, Astarte,

---

*The Book of Abramelin tells the story of an Egyptian mage named Abraham (ca. 1362– ca. 1458) who taught magic to Abraham of Worms.

Diana. The Cretan name of Diana was Diktynna, and as such the goddess wore a wreath made of this magic plant. The Dihtamnon is an evergreen shrub whose contact, as claimed in Occultism, develops and at the same time cures somnambulism. Mixed with Verbena it will produce clairvoyance and ecstasy. Pharmacy attributes to the Dihtamnon strongly sedative and quieting properties. It grows in abundance on Mount Dicte, in Crete, and enters into many magical performances resorted to by the Cretans even to this day.[8]

Dittany of Crete is antibacterial, antifungal, and antimicrobial. Simmer the flowering tops and leaves in ale or wine with Vervain (*Verbena hastata, V. officinalis*), Hyssop (*Hyssopus officinalis*), and American Pennyroyal (*Hedeoma pulegioides*) or Pennyroyal (*Mentha pulegium*) to make a tea that can allay the pains of childbirth. Dittany can also help with cramps, stomach problems, urinary issues, and headaches and may be helpful against gum disease when used as a mouth wash.

Dittany is a sovereign wound herb; simmer the herb or roots to make a fomentation for sprains, bruises, and rheumatic pain.

CAUTION: Dittany is an emmenagogue and should be avoided in pregnancy. Avoid also during breastfeeding. The fresh herb may increase photosensitivity in the skin upon contact. Use internally as medicine for no more than 1 to 2 weeks.

Dittany of Crete at Samhain
Put Dittany tea or tincture into the ritual cup. Burn it as incense or strew it on the ritual fire.

Elder
(*Sambucus* spp.)

Place Elder sprigs in the coffin.

For more on the lore, history, and usage of Elder, see page 27.

Hawthorn, May Tree, Whitethorn
(*Crataegus* spp.)

In Scandinavian tradition, Hawthorn is sacred to the god Thor and the wood was once used in funeral pyres so the spirit of the deceased could escape via the burning thorns and ascend to the celestial realms. (Hawthorns in bloom smell like rotting flesh, a strategy used to attract the flies and bees that pollinate them, which may be a reason they were strongly associated with death.)

Hawthorns are used to decorate the top of Maypoles in traditional British Beltaine celebrations because the blooming of the Hawthorn marks the official start of summer. The tree blooms only when all danger of frost is over, and the blossoms signal that it is safe to move the cows to their summer pastures.

In Irish tradition, Hawthorn belongs to the fairies, and Hawthorn is said to be the sentinel at the gateway between this world and the Otherworld of the sidhe. Any solitary Hawthorn growing on a hill, especially if there is a water source nearby, is sure to be an entrance to the land of fairies. A farmer with a solitary Hawthorn in his field is considered to be especially blessed—though not all encounters with fairies have happy endings.

> One such example (of many) comes from Sir Samuel Ferguson's "The Fairy Tree," where a group of maidens sneak out to dance on a hill with the hawthorn (the fairy tree), ashes, and rowans. They slow down and quickly fall asleep and are enchanted, "For, from the air above, the grassy ground beneath, and from the mountain-ashes and the old Whitehorn between, a Power of faint enchantment doth through their beings breathe, and they sink down together on the green." The fairies come to visit them (and I'm not talking about Walt Disney fairies here), and one of their number, Anna Grace, is taken away and never seen again.[9]

The Irish consider it very bad luck to mess with a Hawthorn.

Earlier in the [twentieth] century, a construction firm ordered the felling of a fairy thorn on a building site in Downpatrick, Ulster. The foreman had to do the deed himself, as all of his workers refused. When he dug up the root, hundreds of white mice*—supposed to be the faeries themselves—ran out, and while the foreman was carting away the soil in a barrow, a nearby horse shied, crushing him against a wall and resulting in the loss of one of his legs.

Even as recently as 1982, workers in the De Lorean car plant in Northern Ireland claimed that one of the reasons the business had so many problems was because a faery thorn bush had been disturbed during the construction of the plant. The management took this so seriously that they actually had a similar bush brought in and planted with all due ceremony![10]

Celtic bards once stood under a Hawthorn tree to utter curses. The Uraicecht Na Ríar (The Poetic Grades of Early Irish Law) includes a description of the magical technique for composing a *glám dícenn* (a poet's black magic). The poet composed the satire in the shade of a flowering Hawthorn tree with no thorns and a dense, heavy top. The satire had to be repeated three-times-nine times, in the "circuit of the moon" (possibly over a one-month period). While chanting, the poet had to pierce a clay likeness of the person being satirized with thorns.

Hawthorn has countless medicinal uses. The tea of the flowers and young leaves makes a gargle for sore throats. The spring leaves and flowers and the fall-gathered berries (pick after the first frost, when they are red and fully ripe) are tinctured to make a heart tonic that can benefit high or low blood pressure, atherosclerosis, irregular heartbeat, and elevated cholesterol levels.

The berries are simmered to make a tea for sore throats, indigestion, anxiety, and menstrual issues. Apply the brew externally as a wash for boils, sores, ulcers, itching, and frostbite.

---

*In Celtic belief, white animals are a sign from the Otherworld.

CAUTION: Do not use Hawthorn with other cardiac medicines (I have seen a precipitous drop in blood pressure from this, several times). It may cause nausea, stomach upset, fatigue, sweating, headache, dizziness, heart palpitations, nosebleeds, insomnia, agitation, and other problems in some individuals. It should probably be avoided during pregnancy and breastfeeding.[11]

Following are recipes for Hawthorn jam and chutney. Both use the berries, which you should gather in the fall after the first frost, when they are bright red and ripe. Hawthorns belong to the fairies, who use them to mark the entrance to their underground dwellings. The fairy realm and the ancestral realm of the dead are essentially the same place. Hawthorn berries ripen just in time for the Samhain feast, so why not make use of them?

🍃 Hawthorn Jam*

You'll need paraffin wax to seal the jars of jam. Melt it in a double boiler and keep it warm while you prepare the berries.

> 3 quarts hawthorn berries
>
> 1–2 lemons, sliced
>
> 1 cup water
>
> 3 tablespoons fruit pectin
>
> 5 cups raw, organic honey

Rinse the berries and remove any stems.

Simmer the berries and lemon in the water until soft, about 45 minutes. Mash the cooked berries slightly with a potato masher. Squeeze out the juice through cheesecloth or muslin (or allow to drip gently overnight through a colander lined with cheesecloth if you want a clearer jelly).

Bring the liquid to a quick boil over high heat. Add the fruit pectin to the hot mixture and combine well. Add the honey and boil for 1 minute.

Remove from the heat and seal by spooning into sterilized jars with clean, hot lids and hot water bath can for 15 minutes, or keep in the refrigerator for up to 3 months.

---

*Adapted from Ellen Evert Hopman, *Tree Medicine Tree Magic* (Los Angeles, Calif.: Pendraig Publishing, 2017), 7.

🍂 Hawthorn Berry Chutney*

Hawthorn chutney is nice to serve with bread and cheese or with cold meats. Consider it for your Dumb Supper as a seasonally appropriate condiment.

> 4.5 pounds ripe hawthorn berries (gathered after the first frost, when they are fully red)
>
> 1 quart organic apple cider vinegar
>
> 2 tablespoons sea salt
>
> A few sprigs of organic, fresh thyme
>
> 2¾ cups organic brown sugar
>
> 2 tablespoons ground ginger
>
> 1 tablespoon ground nutmeg
>
> ½ tablespoon ground cloves
>
> ½ tablespoon ground allspice
>
> ½ teaspoon black pepper

Place the berries in a 6-quart pot, add the apple cider vinegar and sea salt and bring to a boil. Turn down the heat to simmer, cover, and cook the berries until soft—about 45 minutes. Then mash the berries slightly with a potato masher.

Rub the berries through a sieve into a clean pot (the idea is to remove the seeds). Remove the stems from the leaves of the thyme, chop, and add the thyme to the pot along with the sugar and spices. Cook for 10 minutes on medium heat until the sugar is completely melted, stirring constantly.

Spoon the hawthorn berry chutney into sterilized jars, put on clean, hot lids, and hot water bath can for 15 minutes, or store in the refrigerator for up to 3 months.

---

*Adapted from Suzanne Talbert's "Recipe: Hawthorn Chutney," Cedar Mountain Herb School (website).

Hawthorn Tree at Samhain

Sleep or perform a rite under a Hawthorn tree and you may see fairies. Add some dry Hawthorn branches to the ritual fire. If you have a species of Hawthorn with large thorns, bore a hole into the blunt end of the thorn and, with red thread, use the thorn to sew a spell into a piece of natural linen or cotton cloth. Hang the cloth in a tree. As the cloth rots, the spell will be released.

Lotus
(Nelumbo nucifera)

A true spiritual elixir revered by the ancient Egyptians, Lotus is burned as incense to encourage the dead to seek their highest reincarnation. The scent reminds the living of our own divinity and teaches us to move through life without attachment to possessions and cares. Notice how Lotus floats upon the water and no drop of water sticks to it. It thrives in murky ponds, floating serenely above the muck and grime.

> This plant is known to be associated with rebirth. This is a consequence of it supposedly retracting into the water at the night, and emerging a fresh in the sun the next day. . . . The Egyptians therefore associated the lotus flower with the sun which also disappeared in the night, only to re-emerge in the morning. Therefore, the lotus came to symbolize the sun and the creation. In many hieroglyphic works the lotus is depicted as emerging from Nun (the primordial water) bearing the sun god.
>
> As something that is associated with rebirth, it is no surprise that the lotus flower is also associated with death, and the famous Egyptian Book of the Dead is known to include spells that are able to transform a person into a lotus, thus allowing for resurrection.[12]

Osiris was the grandson and favorite of the sun god Ra, and the first pharaoh of Egypt. His brother, Set, was jealous of Osiris's status and murdered him in a fit of jealousy, after which he cut up Osiris's body and threw the pieces into the Nile. Osiris's wife, the goddess Isis, found Osiris's body parts within a great tree* and used her magic and power to bring her husband back to life. Then Ra made him the royal ruler of the dead. Osiris and Isis bore a son, Horus (Horus the Younger), known as the god of the newborn sun, implying that he was reborn each year at

---

*Some sources claim that the tree was a Tamarind (*Tamarindus indica*), but it could also have been a Sycamore Fig (*Ficus sycomorus*), a tree from which Egyptian mummy cases were made. (See E. W. G. Masterman's "Sycomore, Tree" entry in the International Standard Bible Encyclopedia Online, 2018. Originally published in 1939 by Wm. B. Eerdmans Publishing Co.)

the winter solstice. Images of Horus sometimes show him seated upon a Lotus blossom. Just as Osiris dies and is re-membered by Isis each year, Horus is reborn each year at the Solstice. Winter solstice is the time of the death of the old year and the rebirth of the new sun cycle, and the Lotus was a symbol of death and rebirth in ancient Egyptian thinking. The Lotus is born in the muck and darkness of a pond, yet rises above to become the most beautiful of flowers. Nothing sticks to it once it emerges, even water can only bead up on its leaves. Lotus flowers close at night and open again in the sunlight of the morning, symbolizing rebirth, re-creation, and enlightenment.

> As a symbol of re-birth, the lotus was closely related to the imagery of the funerary and Osirian cult. The Four Sons of Horus were frequently shown standing on a lotus in front of Osiris. The Book of the Dead contains spells for "transforming oneself into a lotus" and thus fulfilling the promise of resurrection.[13]

In records of ancient Egyptian religion and on architecture of the period, the Lotus appears frequently. It is one of the most important symbols with connotations of death, rebirth, and immortality. The Egyptian Book of the Dead offers a spell for transforming into a Lotus: "I am this pure lotus which went forth from the sunshine, which is at the nose of Re; I have descended that I may seek it for Horus, for I am the pure one who issued from the fen."[14] Once again we are reminded of the life pattern of Lotus, which rises from the dank marshes to become a glorious flower that floats serenely on the murky waters, unsullied, setting an example for how to behave in life and in death. If we are as pure as the Lotus, we can dwell in the realm of Osiris for all time.

A spell giving praise to Osiris, the Lord of Eternity, from the Book of the Dead is paired with a Papyrus painting showing a lady worshipping Osiris, holding Papyrus flowers and a sistrum and wearing a Lotus flower on her head: "My heart comes to you bearing truth, my heart has no falseness. May you grant that I be among the living and that I fare downstream and upstream in your land."[15]

Medicinally, Lotus strengthens the kidneys and the heart. The leaf is used for fever and diarrhea and can counteract alcohol or mushroom poisoning. The bud is used to calm worry and anxiety, for insomnia, and to lower fevers. The seeds are used for insomnia, heart palpitations, and chronic diarrhea.

CAUTION: Lotus can lower blood sugar levels and should be avoided (or used with great caution) by diabetics. Women who are pregnant or breastfeeding should avoid it. Stop using it 2 weeks before a planned surgery.[16]

Lotus at Samhain
Place a Lotus flower on the altar. Meditate on birth, death, and rebirth.

Marjoram
(Origanum majorana)

The genus name *Origanum* comes from the Greek *oros* and *ganos,* meaning "joy of the mountains."[17] Indeed, the Greeks and Romans considered Marjoram to be an herb of happiness and love, and they planted it on graves to bring joy and peace to the deceased. Plant the herb around the house and use the essential oil or drink the tea to dispel grief.

Sweet marjoram has long been an herb of love. According to Roman legend, the goddess of love, Venus, gave the plant its scent "to remind mortals of her beauty." A similar legend surrounds Aphrodite, Venus's counterpart in Greek mythology, who is said to have created sweet marjoram and grew it on Mount Olympus. Marjoram has been used in love potions and spells and as a wedding herb in nosegays/tussie mussies and bridal bouquets. In ancient Greece and Rome, a crown of marjoram was worn by the bride and groom during wedding ceremonies, a tradition that has also been associated with wild marjoram/oregano. . . . In addition to its association with Aphrodite and Venus, marjoram was reportedly worn during rites to the god Osiris in ancient Egypt. . . . Wild marjoram also has an association with spirits, as it was thought to "help the dead sleep peacefully" if planted on a grave and foretell a happy afterlife if found growing on a grave in Greece.[18]

In ancient Egypt, Marjoram was sacred to the crocodile god, Sobek, son of Neith, creatrix of the universe. Sobek was sometimes considered to be an aspect of Horus because Horus took the form of a crocodile to retrieve the parts of Osiris's body that were lost in the Nile, and Sobek was also thought to have assisted Isis in the birth of Horus.[19] Offerings to Sobek often included eggs, statues of crocodiles, crocodile teeth, warm incense, spices, resins, and, among other herbs, Marjoram and Oregano (*Origanum vulgare*).[20]

In modern times, a drop or two of Marjoram essential oil can be placed on a sore tooth to relieve pain (take no more than 2 drops per day). It is also used for coughs, gallbladder pain, depression, migraine, digestive disorders, headaches, coughs, colds, and nerve pain, as a compress, in a diffuser, in liniments, and so on.

The herbal tea brings on perspiration, helping to lower a fever. It can benefit liver disease, stomach ailments such as gas and cramps, and menopausal symptoms, and it helps bring in breast milk. The tea is also used for colic, headache, earache, and cough and is safe for young children. It is a tonic for the heart and nerves and can improve insomnia, muscle spasms, back pain, and blood circulation.

Use the plant externally to make a fomentation for rheumatism and swollen joints.

CAUTION: Marjoram is an emmenagogue so it should be avoided in pregnancy. Long-term use of it could cause cancer. Children should avoid ingestion of the oil. Some people will experience contact dermatitis when using the fresh herb on their skin or in their eyes. Test a small area of skin before you apply it.[21]

Marjoram at Samhain

Plant Marjoram on the grave of a loved one or in your garden. Use it in a dish for your Samhain feast or Dumb Supper (chopped fresh

Marjoram is nice sprinkled on a salad, on deviled eggs, in sausages, in tomato dishes, and on poultry and game).

Marsh Mallow
(Althaea officinalis)

Gentle Marsh Mallow attracts benevolent spirits and bestows protection from prickly curses. Place a bowl of its leaves and flowers on your altar or tuck it into skulls and power bundles. Make a salve of Marsh Mallow and Rosemary (*Rosmarinus officinalis*) and anoint yourself with it when doing trance work or summoning spirits.* You can also add herbs like Lavender (*Lavandula angustifolia*), Eucalyptus (*Eucalyptus* spp.), Comfrey (*Symphytum officinale*), Plantain (*Plantago major*), Calendula (*Calendula officinalis*), or Saint John's Wort (*Hypericum perforatum*). The salve would also be useful for healing sores, inflammations, sunburn, itching, and other skin discomforts.

In Voodoo practice, Marsh Mallow is said to be not only a good "spirit puller" (attracting good spirits) but also a "love puller" (attracting love). Traditionally, herbalist Crystal Aneira tells us, "it is burned on charcoal with Apple and Rose blossoms to invite a marriage proposal." She also suggest that if you carry Marsh Mallow root or leaf together with Angelica root (*Angelica archangelica*) in a white flannel bag, "unseen helping hands will protect you from evil, illness, and sorrow."[22]

In *Plant Lore, Legends and Lyrics*, Richard Folkard notes, "According to a German tradition, an ointment made of the leaves of the Marsh Mallow was employed to anoint the body of anyone affected by witchcraft"[23]—and thus undo any spell craft, we presume.

Marsh Mallow is greatly valued for its medicinal uses. Its leaves and root are demulcent—that is, soothing to the mucous linings—for the throat, respiratory tract, stomach, bowels, and bladder. They are also anti-inflammatory and can be applied as a poultice to infections, ulcers, burns, sunburn, insect bites, itching, and sores. Add the roots and leaves to salves for the skin.

---

*Herbalist Sarah Anne Lawless has a recipe for a Marsh Mallow and Rosemary salve on her website (sarahannelawless.com).

> **CAUTION:** Marsh Mallow can have unpredictable effects on blood sugar levels; diabetics should monitor their blood sugar levels when using this herb. Women who are pregnant or breastfeeding should avoid it. Discontinue use before surgery.

Marsh Mallow at Samhain

Wear a crown of the leaves and anoint yourself with a Marsh Mallow ointment before the rite. Place dishes of it on the altar to attract friendly spirits. Add the roots to syrups and elixirs and incorporate those into your ceremony.

Mullein
(Verbascum thapsus)

For lore, history, and usage of Mullein, see page 43. Mullein is used in potions to see into the Otherworld and to communicate with its denizens and is an aid to prophetic or lucid dreaming and Astral travel. Combine Mullein flowers with Mugwort and Mint leaves to make a dreaming tea. Made into incense with Dittany of Crete and inhaled, Mullein will open the third eye so you can more easily see the spirits.

Note Mullein, which here is called by its Latin variant *Tapsus barbatus,* in this list of herbs to communicate with the spirits from *The Philosophy of Natural Magic,* by German Occultist Heinrich Cornelius Agrippa von Nettesheim (1486–1535).

> There are also suffumigations under opportune influences of the Stars that make the images of spirits forthwith appear in the air or elsewhere. So, they say, that if of coriander, smallage, henbane, and hemlock, be made a fume, that spirits will presently come together; hence they are called spirit's herbs. Also, it is said, that fume made of the root of the reedy herb sagapen, with the juice of hemlock and henbane, and the herb tapsus barbatus, red sanders, and black poppy, makes spirits and strange shapes appear.[24]

Myrrh
(Commiphora myrrha)

Myrrh is associated with death and resurrection and was used in ancient Egyptian embalming mixtures. It is said to bring peace; it aids in meditation and can be burned as incense to consecrate an area. Myrrh is sacred to Isis, the goddess of death and mourning.

> Myrrh's bitterness may easily be associated with Isis' bitter task of searching for the scattered pieces of Her beloved husband's body. In the magical papyri, myrrh is called the Guide of Isis for it was thought to assist Her in this sorrowful task. While the papyri don't say specifically how Isis employed Her "guide," we can speculate that She may have burned it as incense—perhaps as part of a visionary rite—or made it into ink with which to inscribe amulets to aid Her search. A recipe for one such magical ink included myrrh, along with dried figs, date pits, and wormwood. The ritual instructions tell us that this ink was the one Isis used to record Her magical words as She fit together the members of Osiris. Myrrh was also sometimes called the Tears of Horus, perhaps in connection with His own mourning for His father.[25]

This parable tells us that Myrrh has profound associations with death and rebirth and is a fitting incense to use as we communicate with those who have crossed the veil and with the deities of those realms. It is also one of the sacred herbs that was offered to all Egyptian deities as in this hymn to Isis at her temple in Philae: "O Isis, giver of life who dwells in the Pure Island, take to yourself the myrrh which comes from Punt, the lotus-fragrance which issues from your body, that your heart may be glad through it, and that your heart may rejoice every day."[26]

This quote from a collection of Greco-Egyptian magical texts known as The Greek Magical Papyri (Latin *Papyri Graecae Magicae*), an assemblage of spells, formulas, hymns, and rituals dating from 100s BC to the 400s AD, shows us Myrrh's connection to dusk—the sun disappearing into the Western ocean has long been associated with its descent to the Land of the Dead: ". . . frankincense belongs to the solar god/s, while myrrh belongs to Selene.* . . . Frankincense is sacrificed at dawn, and then myrrh at evening."[27]

Myrrh is renowned for its use in incense, religious ritual, and magic, but it also has medicinal uses. The tea and alcohol tincture of the resin are used to strengthen the heart and circulation and can benefit indigestion, ulcers, colds, coughs, asthma, lung congestion, arthritis pain, cancer, leprosy, spasms, and syphilis, and it is also used to increase menstrual flow. *To make the tea:* Steep 1 teaspoon of powdered resin in 1 cup of just-boiled water for 15 minutes. Drink 3 times daily, not with meals.

The tea can also be used as a disinfectant wound wash and to heal hemorrhoids, bedsores, and boils. Be careful to first remove any dirt from the wound because Myrrh will seal up the area very quickly. If you don't have the time or wherewithal to make tea, you can apply the powdered herb directly to the wound.

> **CAUTION: Some people may experience a skin rash with external use of Myrrh, or diarrhea with internal use. Using Myrrh in large amounts or for a prolonged period could lead to kidney or heart damage. Women who are pregnant or breastfeeding should avoid it. Myrrh may lower blood sugar levels and should not be used together with medications that lower blood sugar. It could make a fever, uterine bleeding, or systemic inflammation worse. Stop its use 2 weeks before a scheduled surgery.[28]**

Myrrh at Samhain
Burn Myrrh on Samhain Eve on the altar or on a grave as a hallowed offering to the realm of the dead and to the deities who live there. It is one of their preferred fragrances.

---

*Selene is the moon goddess, also known as Luna.

Parsley
(Petroselinum crispum)

Parsley is sacred to the goddess Persephone. It was planted on graves in her honor and used in Greek funeral rites, wound into funeral wreaths and used to decorate tombs because of its association with the hero god Archemorous, the herald of death. Greek lore held that Parsley grew where his blood seeped into the ground after serpents devoured him. It was Persephone who guided the souls of the dead to the Underworld and Persephone had come to collect Archemorous's spirit in the form of Parsley. Also, according to Greek legend, Parsley must visit with Hades, Persephone's husband and the god of the Underworld, nine times before it will germinate.

> [In Rome] when funeral games were played, participating athletes donned wreaths of parsley. Romans would create these wreaths for their own funerals and adorn their graves with them. It was believed that great fields of parsley grew on Ogygia, the death island of Calypso. There was also the saying, *De'eis thai selinon*—"to need only parsley," which was a gentle way of saying someone had "one foot in the grave."[29]

Medicinally, Parsley root and leaf tea helps asthma and coughs and is a diuretic for milder kidney issues. A decoction of the seeds can relieve fever. Externally, the leaves are used to poultice cancers and insect bites and stings. The fresh juice is applied to sore eyes and to conjunctivitis and blepharitis. Eat more parsley to improve your eyesight.

CAUTION: Eating large amounts of Parsley leaves or seeds (very large amounts; Parsley is perfectly safe for culinary use) can damage your kidneys and may cause abortion or fetal birth defects. Diabetics take note: It can lower blood sugar levels, so monitor carefully. Parsley could worsen edema and high blood pressure. Stop using it 2 weeks before a planned surgery.[30]

Parsley at Samhain

Make a crown of Parsley and wear it to your Samhain ritual. Plant Parsley on a grave. Make a Parsley wreath and hang it on the door. Decorate dishes of food for the Samhain feast with sprigs of fresh Parsley.

Pasqueflower, Pulsatilla
(*Anemone pulsatilla*)

Pulsatilla is said to have grown from the tears of Venus as she wept for the dead Adonis, and the manner in which the plant's flower-heads droop and sway in the wind does seem mournful. Perhaps that explains, at least in part, why it was planted on graves in ancient Greece.

> According to Frazer's 'The Golden Bough,' the herb was first cre-ated from droplets of Adonis' blood, when he was gored by a wild boar on Mount Lebanon, a highly significant event in the mythic cycles of the Phoenicians, and one which happens every year accord-ing to their calendar. . . . The herb has a long association with the faerie folk, with rural people believing that the maturing flower was the perfect nesting place for fair folk. The flower petals close at sun-down, so the plant has also gained the legend that woodland fairies shelter beneath the plant's petals at night.[31]

The tincture of the aerial parts of the flowering plant is used (in very small amounts) for digestive and lung conditions. It helps with coughs, bronchitis, asthma, whooping cough, nervous exhaustion, and mucous conditions of the eye.

Pulsatilla is also suited for use with the reproductive organs; it helps with painful testicles, painful ovaries, and painful menstrual cramps. It can also be used to treat insomnia, headaches, earaches, and nerve pain.

Make a poultice of the herb to treat boils, skin infections, and inflammation.

CAUTION: Try a small amount of Pulsatilla before applying it to the skin; for some people it is an allergen and a severe irritant. Women who are pregnant or breastfeeding should avoid it. For teas, use only the dried plant, as the fresh herb can be harsh. For tinctures, take no more than 2 or 3 drops, diluted in water, 3 or 4 times a day. Overdosing can be dangerous or even fatal. However, homeopathic dilutions are quite safe for internal use.[32]

Pulsatilla at Samhain

Plant some Pulsatilla to please the fairies and give them a nesting place. These perennials like well-drained, alkaline soil with full to partial sun.

Periwinkle
(Vinca minor, V. major)

Periwinkle, a common woodland groundcover, is also known as Sorcerer's Violet, Flower of Immortality, and Flower of Death, which gives us a hint about its magical reputation. It is said to be a charm against evil spirits, and wearing the herb or hanging it over the door and on gateposts will repel both evil spirits and ill-intentioned sorcery.

In France, periwinkle was regarded as a symbol of friendship, and if the plant was placed in a buttonhole it was thought to keep evil spirits away. In some areas, it was added to both wedding and funeral wreaths.

In Italy, the plant was usually associated with death, and it was often placed on top of caskets of dead children. Also, wreaths bound by periwinkle were once placed around the neck of condemned men, before their execution.[33]

Periwinkle likes to grow on disturbed ground, which may be why it favors graves. When found growing on a grave, especially that of a child, it enables the parents to maintain their connection with the child's eternal spirit.

Vinca minor and *V. major* have the same medicinal properties. A tea of the herb and flower is used for diarrhea, gastritis, heavy menstruation, and bleeding between periods and other hemorrhages, and as a gargle for tonsillitis and sore throat. Periwinkle is sedative and beneficial for nervous conditions.

Externally, the tea is used as a wash for eczema, wounds, and inflammations. A poultice of the plant can help with cramps. Use it in salves for hemorrhoids and for inflammations.

> CAUTION: Taking large amounts of Periwinkle could harm the kidneys and nervous system, upset digestion, and cause hypertension. Avoid during pregnancy and breastfeeding. Periwinkle can cause skin irritation in some people.[34]

Periwinkle at Samhain

Make a wreath of Periwinkle and hang it on your door. Drape it over gates and windowsills as protection against ill-intentioned spirits. Place a vase of Periwinkles on the altar, in memory of a deceased child.

Pine
(*Pinus* spp.)

Pine represents peace and immortality, and its wood is traditionally used to make coffins. For example, in Orthodox Jewish tradition, the coffin is ideally made with just Pine and kosher glue, with no metal, using wooden dowels instead of nails.

In their Great Symbols series, the Theosophy Trust notes, "the pine is a powerful and organically complete symbol of an axis linking the three worlds of heaven, earth and Hades. This is why the pine is called both the tree of life and of death and is used as a means of communicating with the highest gods as well as with the dead, or what the Estonians and Finns would call *Hiisi,* spirits of the underground. . . . The Votiaks of Siberia also leave sacrificial offerings in pine trees out of the same concern to communicate with spirits of the earth and of their own ancient heroes. It is as though the branches bear the offering which will be transmitted in spirit to the roots."[35]

For more on the lore, history, and usage of Pine, see page 30.

Rosemary
(*Rosmarinus officinalis*)

A traditional herb for purification and remembrance, Rosemary helps us both honor the memory of our dead and protect against ill-intentioned energies that can arise from the Otherworld as our loved ones pass over. In medieval and Renaissance times, Rosemary was added to bridal wreaths, worn or carried during a funeral, cast onto the coffin and grave, and burned to protect the home from disease and evil spirits.

Commenting on the dual uses of Rosemary in wedding bouquets and for funerals poet Robert Herrick writes:

> *Grow for two ends—it matters not at all*
> *Be't for my bridall, or my buriall.*

> ROBERT HERRICK,
> FROM "THE ROSEMARY BRANCH"

Ancient Greek scholars wore Rosemary in their hair so they could better memorize for their exams. William Shakespeare echoes that practice in *Hamlet* (act 4, scene 5), when he has Ophelia say: "There's rosemary, that's for remembrance. Pray you, love, remember." In reference to the English tradition of strewing Rosemary on a corpse and grave, Shakespeare penned this line in *Romeo and Juliet* (act 4, scene 5): "Dry up your tears and stick your rosemary / On this fair corse, and, as the custom is, / And in her best array, bear her to church."

In Sicily, it is said that the young fairies lie concealed under its branches in the guise of snakes. And this bit of sage advice comes from the British herbal tradition: "Where rosemary flourishes, the lady rules."

In herbal medicine, the tea of the leaf and flower is used to stimulate the liver and digestion and boost circulation. It is known to relieve depression, gout, migraine, and headaches, to slightly lower blood pressure, to aid with memory loss, and to benefit breast and colon cancers.[36]

The tea makes a mouthwash for bad breath and is used in perfumes and colognes (with Lavender and Myrtle) such as the Queen of

Hungary's Water. Massage the tea or oil into the scalp to promote hair growth. Eczema, joint pain, muscle pain, and sciatica are helped with washes, rubs, and fomentations of this plant; the washes and salves of Rosemary can help heal wounds.

Steep the plant in white wine for a week and massage the wine into gouty or paralyzed limbs to stimulate blood flow and invigorate tissues. When drunk, the wine quiets the heart and stimulates the kidneys, brain, and nervous system.

CAUTION: Though culinary amounts are perfectly safe, large doses or prolonged use of Rosemary could be fatal. Women who are pregnant should avoid using it in medicinal doses. The essential oil is too strong for internal use and could harm the kidneys and uterus and cause photosensitivity. Seizure disorders and bleeding disorders can be made worse by this herb. Avoid it if you are allergic to aspirin.[37]

A decoction of Rosemary can be used in the bath, as a hair rinse, and in lotions and creams. Rosemary fights skin-damaging free radicals, promotes healthy cell development, and has properties to kill bacteria, fungi, and viruses on the skin, making it valuable to help heal minor wounds and burns, dermatitis, acne, eczema, and psoriasis. A Rosemary hair rinse can help with itchy scalp and dandruff. Those with darker shades of hair will appreciate it as it will even darken grayer shades.

🍃 Rosemary Hair Rinse

Use this as your final rinse after shampooing and conditioning the hair.

> 3 cups water
> 2 fresh rosemary sprigs or 1 tablespoon dried organic
>   Rosemary
> 1 teaspoon aloe vera gel

Steep the rosemary in 3 cups of boiling hot water for 20 minutes. Allow the tea to cool, then strain into a large glass jar. Add the aloe vera gel and cap tightly. Keeps for about 1 week in a cool, dark place.

🍃 Rosemary Facial Toner*

> 2 cups water
>
> 2 sprigs of fresh organic rosemary or 1 tablespoon dried organic rosemary
>
> 3 tablespoons organic apple cider vinegar (or half witch hazel and half apple cider vinegar)

Combine the water and rosemary in a pot and bring to a boil, then turn down to simmer until the liquid is reduced by half. Remove from the heat and allow to cool. Strain into a glass jar and add the apple cider vinegar. Cap tightly.

Keeps about 6 months when kept in a cool, dark place.

---

*Adapted from Andrea's "Homemade Facial Toner with Rosemary," Homemade for Elle (website), February 26, 2014.

Rosemary Facial Cream*

> ½ ounce white, cosmetic-grade bee's wax
>
> 3 ounces almond oil
>
> 3 tablespoons strong rosemary tea (made with flowers, stems, and leaves, just barely covered with water and simmered for about 5 minutes, then allowed to cool)
>
> ¼ teaspoon powdered borax

Combine the wax and oil in a double boiler or bain-marie. Heat and stir gently until they are well mixed.

Combine the rosemary water and borax in a separate pan. Heat and stir gently until the borax dissolves. Slowly combine the two mixtures, stirring all the while. Remove from the flame and whip until the mixture turns creamy. Let cool, then transfer to pots or small jars. Cap and use within 3 weeks.

---

*Adapted from Pamela Michael, *A Country Harvest* (New York: Exeter Books, 1987), 155.

Rosemary at Samhain

Burn Rosemary in the ritual fire in remembrance of a deceased ancestor. Place it on the altar and add it to dishes for the feast.

Star Anise, Chinese Star Anise
(*Illicium verum*)

The powdered bark of Star Anise is used in incense mixtures, which can be used in ceremonies to honor the dead.

The Japanese plant a close relative of Star Anise, which they call *shikimi-no-ki* (*Illicium anisatum*), around temples and graves to protect and consecrate the area. They also decorate graves with branches of this plant, possibly because it is poisonous and would ward off animals.

On Mexico's Día de los Muertos (Day of the Dead), an ancient festival that long predates European colonization, Pan de Muerto (Bread of the Dead) is baked and shaped into skulls or round loaves with dough strips on top that resemble bones. Pan de Muerto is served in local cafes and included in *ofrendas,* which are collections of the favorite foods of deceased ancestors placed on an altar or grave to honor them. The bread traditionally contains Anise seeds (*Pimpinella anisum*), and it can also be made with Star Anise, which has a similar flavor.

Pan de Muerto Bread*

> ¼ cup organic milk
>
> ¼ cup organic butter
>
> ¼ cup warm water
>
> 3 cups organic all-purpose flour, divided
>
> 1¼ teaspoons active dry yeast
>
> ½ teaspoon sea salt
>
> 1 teaspoon ground star anise seed or 2 teaspoons anise seed
> or ½ teaspoon anise extract (they are different plants and
> star anise has a stronger flavor than anise seed)
>
> ¼ cup organic white sugar (or ⅛ cup raw, local honey)
>
> 2 free-range, organic eggs, beaten
>
> 2 teaspoons organic orange zest

Heat the milk and the butter together in a saucepan until the butter melts. Remove from the heat and add the warm water. The mixture should be around 110°F.

---

*Adapted from Lola's Pan de Muertos (Mexican Bread of the Dead), AllRecipes.com.

In a large bowl combine 1 cup of the flour, yeast, sea salt, star anise seed, and sugar. Beat this into the warm milk mixture. Add the eggs and orange zest and beat until well mixed. Stir in ½ cup of flour and continue adding more flour until the dough is soft.

Turn the dough out onto a lightly floured surface and knead until smooth and elastic. Place the dough into a lightly greased bowl, cover with plastic wrap, and let rise in a warm place until doubled in size. (This will take about 1 to 2 hours).

Punch down the dough and shape it into a skull-shaped loaf. Place the dough onto a baking sheet, loosely cover with plastic wrap, and let rise in a warm place for about 1 hour (or until just about doubled in size).

Bake in a preheated 350°F (175°C) oven for about 35 to 45 minutes. Remove from oven, let cool slightly, then brush with glaze.

Glaze for the Bread

> ¼ cup organic white sugar
> ¼ cup organic orange juice
> 1 tablespoon orange zest
> 2 tablespoons organic white sugar

In a small saucepan combine the ¼ cup sugar, orange juice, and orange zest. Bring to a boil over medium heat and boil for 2 minutes.

Brush over the top of the bread while it's still warm. Sprinkle the glazed bread with 2 tablespoons white sugar.

The seeds of Chinese Star Anise (not the poisonous Japanese Star Anise!) are used in medicine. Chew the seeds or make a decoction of them to aid digestion. Use them in teas for colic, rheumatic cramps, nausea, or insomnia and to build breast milk. They are sometimes used to treat coughs, bronchitis, and flu.

The seeds also have an affinity for the reproductive tract; they bring on menstruation, ease childbirth, and increase sex drive in men.

You can make a pleasant-tasting tincture of the seeds in brandy with some organic lemon peel and let steep for a week. Take in ¼-teaspoon doses for coughs, colds, cramps, and so on.

The powdered seeds are added to salves for scabies and lice.

> **CAUTION: Some people may experience contact dermatitis from Star Anise. Unfortunately, it is sometimes adulterated with its poisonous cousin, Japanese Star Anise (*Illicium anisatum*), which can cause seizures and vomiting, so women who are pregnant or breastfeeding and children should avoid it.**[38]

Star Anise at Samhain

Place Star Anise on the altar to honor the dead, or leave some on a grave. Bake a Pan de Muertos and eat it in the cemetery, near the resting place of your ancestor. Leave one on the grave as an offering.

Tansy
(*Tanacetum vulgare*)

Tansy is insecticidal and was once used to wrap meat as a preservative. In ancient Greece, cadavers were wrapped in Tansy while awaiting burial. During the Middle Ages, it was used as a strewing herb to repel flies, moths, and other insect pests, and it was placed around corn stacks to repel rats.[39]

In addition to its practical applications with the dead, tansy is associated with immortality and longevity.

The name "tanacetum" apparently came from the Greek word for immortality, because the flowers take a long time to fade (and perhaps because of the plant's association with the dead). Indeed, when Zeus fell in love with the beautiful young man Ganymede, he was given tansy to make him immortal.[40]

A tea of the dried leaf and flower was once recommended as a remedy to expel worms. While fasting, a person would take one cup at night and another in the next morning.

Tansy is also recommended for intestinal gas, stomachache, ulcers, epileptic seizures, colds, fevers, hysteria, gout, and kidney problems, and it is known to bring on the menses. A single leaf placed in the pot with your regular tea was said to be strengthening to the heart.

The tea was once used externally as a wash for bruises, sores, sprains, itching, and sunburn and as a fomentation or poultice for tumors.

> **CAUTION:** Tansy contains thujone, a toxic chemical, so it should be used with extreme caution. It should not be used in large doses or for an extended period. Overuse of the tea could cause tremors, liver or kidney damage, seizures, or death. Women who are pregnant or breastfeeding should avoid it. Do not ingest the essential oil—it is poisonous. Test it on a small area of skin when first using it, because some people have a severe reaction to it. Those who are allergic to the Aster family of plants should avoid it. It can worsen porphyria.[41]

Tansy at Samhain

As an herb of immortality, Tansy can be placed on the altar to honor the ancestors.

Thyme
(Thymus vulgaris)

Any place where wild Thyme grows is a place of power on the Earth. In the summer months, thyme flowers are alive with bees, said to be the messengers of fairies. It is one of the fairies' favorite flowers, and they like to play in it.

Thyme dispels sorrow and melancholy and facilitates communication with the dead, especially at Samhain. It is said to encourage an easier passage to the afterlife. In Wales it is worn at funerals and planted on graves. The Greeks placed it on coffins at funerals and burned it in their temples as a source of courage.

Medicinally, Thyme is a great lung healer and cleanser. Use a tea of the leaves to dry up coughs and phlegm. Given to women in labor, the tea can also help expel the placenta.

Externally, the tea makes an antiseptic wash for wounds, can relieve swellings and sciatica, and strengthen weak eyes (be sure to filter the tea through a coffee filter before applying to the eyes).

CAUTION: Women who are pregnant or breastfeeding should only use Thyme as food, and not in medicinal quantities. It is a phytoestrogen, meaning it could exacerbate hormone-sensitive conditions and cancers. It also can slow blood clotting, so stop taking it at least 2 weeks before surgery.

Thyme at Samhain

Place a tea or tincture of Thyme into the ritual cup, as well as burn it as incense on the altar. Wear a crown of Thyme as you perform the rite.

Violet
(Viola odorata)

Tiny, unassuming Violets have long been associated with children, probably because of their diminutive size. Violets were traditionally used to make wreaths and crowns for dead children, as a way to honor the deceased, and used to decorate their graves.

> Both Greeks and Romans associated violets with funerals and death. Violets were routinely scattered around tombs, and, as symbols of innocence and modesty, children's graves were routinely so blanketed with violets that the grave was completely covered.[42]

Violet is an edible herb; both the leaves and flowers can be eaten fresh. The leaves can also be cooked, like spinach.

A tea of the leaves can be used for cancer of the colon, throat, or tongue. The flower tea is laxative for adults and children. Tea made from both leaves and flowers is recommended for hot flashes, depression, insomnia, nervous conditions, sore throats, coughs, bronchitis, and digestive complaints.

Add the fresh leaves to healing salves, or use them to make a poultice for wounds or cancers.

> **CAUTION: Violet has no known side effects, but women who are pregnant or breastfeeding should probably use it with caution.**

🌱 Violet Flower Syrup

For this syrup, use the flowers of both Violet (Viola odorata) and Dog Violet (Viola canina). The syrup is laxative and lowers a fever. It is also taken for epilepsy, insomnia, jaundice, sore throats, and headaches.

To make the syrup, pour freshly boiled water over an equal volume of flowers. Steep for 10 hours, then strain.

Reheat the liquid, adding an equal volume of fresh flowers. Let steep for another 10 hours, then strain.

Repeat several more times to produce a very strong tea.

When you are ready, bring the tea to a simmer. Remove from the heat, let cool slightly, and add enough honey, stirring well, until a syrup consistency is reached. Keeps refrigerated for 6 months.

Dosing is 1 to 2 teaspoons for children and 1 tablespoon for adults up to 5 times per day, as needed.

> **CAUTION: Violet Flower Syrup is not for children under 12 months of age.**

Purple is a traditional color of mourning, and purple foods are very appropriate for your Samhain supper.

🌱 Candied Wild Violets*

Make these in the late spring and store the flowers for your Samhain observance. Note that you can use this same process to candy other edible flowers and petals.

 1 free-range, organic egg white, beaten until frothy

 2 tablespoons powdered organic sugar

 20 violet flowers with the stems still attached

_____

*Adapted from Leda Meredith's "Candied Violets," The Spruce Eats (website), November 7, 2018.

Beat the egg white until it is frothy but not stiff. Place the powdered sugar in a sifter (or in a strainer that you can gently tap with your hand to evenly release the sugar).

Pick up a violet flower by the stem. Dip the flower into the egg white, swirling it gently to coat the entire flower. Shake off any excess egg white.

Holding the flower by the stem over a plate, sift the powdered sugar over the flower. Twirl the flower stem between the thumb and forefinger of the hand that is holding it so that the flower gets evenly coated with sugar on all sides (the stem will be cut off later, so just focus on the flower).

Place the violet on a paper towel, resting on a cookie sheet or large plate.

Repeat the egg and sugar steps with the rest of the flowers.

Transfer the sugared flowers on the paper towel to a shelf in your refrigerator. Be sure none of the violets are touching. Leave them uncovered in the refrigerator for 24 hours. As the flowers dry most of the sugar will be absorbed by the egg white, creating a glaze on the petals.

Take the paper towel with the candied flowers on it out of the refrigerator and let it sit out at room temperature in a warm part of your home for another 24 hours.

Snip off the stems and discard them. Transfer the candied violets to an airtight container such as a glass jar with a tight lid. If you need to layer the flowers, place baking paper between each layer to prevent the candied violets from sticking together. Keep in a cool, dry place out of direct sunlight. Use within 2 months.

Alternatively you can place the flowers between layers of waxed paper in a freezer container, seal, label, and freeze for up to 6 months.

Violets at Samhain

Make a dessert and decorate it with candied violets, especially in honor of a dead child. Serve it at your Dumb Supper or Samhain feast.

White Cedar
(Thuja occidentalis)

Burn Cedar during funeral rites to bring peace to those who mourn.

For more on the lore, history, and usage of White Cedar, see page 30.

Wormwood
(*Artemisia absinthium*)

Wormwood forms the base of the classic aperitif absinthe, sometimes called "The Green Fairy" for its hallucinogenic effects. Perhaps because of its mind-opening properties, absinthe was a favorite drink of artists such as Toulouse-Lautrec, Degas, Manet, van Gogh, Picasso, Hemingway, and Oscar Wilde. Pure absinthe is now banned in many countries due to its thujone content. Thujone is a potentially poisonous compound found in Wormwood, and distilling Wormwood in alcohol increases the thujone concentration. In the USA, only absinthe with the thujone removed is legal.

Regarding absinthe, Oscar Wilde wrote:

> After the first glass, you see things as you wish they were. After the second, you see things as they are not. Finally, you see things as they really are, and that is the most horrible thing in the world. . . . Three nights I sat up all night drinking absinthe, and thinking that I was singularly clearheaded and sane. The waiter came in and began watering the sawdust. The most wonderful flowers, tulips, lilies, and roses sprang up and made a garden of the cafe. "Don't you see them?" I said to him. "*Mais, non, monsieur, il n'y a rien.*"[43]

> *The first month of marriage is the honeymoon; the second is the absinthe moon.*
>
> VOLTAIRE

The Latin name for this herb, *Artemisia,* is taken from that of the goddess Artemis. In ancient Greece, Artemis, sister of Apollo, the god of healing, was regarded as the goddess of virgins, childbirth, and girls.

The scent of Wormwood is said to increase psychic powers, and it is burned in the graveyard to summon the spirits of the dead. In the

Germanic tradition, Wormwood was a symbol of grief, and the herb was burned in funeral pyres and left on graves.[44]

Wormwood is said to repel evil spirits, the evil eye, and sorcery. Hang bouquets or bags of the herb on gates and at entrances to protect house and barn. Make a protective wreath of Wormwood and hang it on the door. To fashion a shield against ill-intentioned spirits and baneful Witchcraft, make bundles of Wormwood, Burdock (*Arctium lappa*), Maple (*Acer* spp.), and Alder (*Alnus* spp.) and hang them from the edges of the roof.[45]

Wormwood leaf and flower are used as a tea to aid digestion, improve circulation, benefit the liver, and help with labor pains, irritable bowel syndrome (IBS), fevers, colds, heartburn, mild forms of epilepsy, and muscle spasms. It is a classic herb for pinworm and roundworm. It is somewhat stimulating to the appetite and may be helpful in anorexia nervosa. *Preparation and dosage:* Steep the herb for 10 minutes and take no more than 3 cups in a day.

Make a fomentation of Wormwood for bruises and sprains. It has antibacterial properties and is a good choice for salves and washes for wounds and insect bites. It is helpful in poultices for arthritis and rheumatism thanks to its pain-killing properties.

CAUTION: Excessive use of Wormwood (and of absinthe) can result in headaches, cramps, vomiting, hallucinations, kidney failure, nightmares, paralysis, nerve damage, and even death. Do not use it internally except under expert supervision. Do not take this herb as tea for more than 4 weeks. Women who are pregnant or breastfeeding should avoid it altogether. It can worsen porphyria, kidney problems, and seizure disorders. Do not use with anticonvulsants.

Wormwood at Samhain

Burn it as incense to increase your psychic powers as you seek to communicate with the dead. Hang a protective wreath of Wormwood on doors and gates.

Yew

(*Taxus baccata, T. brevifolia, T. canadensis*)

For lore, history, and usage of Yew, see page 59. The Yew tree was sacred to Hecate, the Greek goddess of crossroads, entranceways, Witchcraft, death, and necromancy. Yew collars were placed on black bulls when they were sacrificed in her honor.

Yew sprays were burned on funeral pyres, and Yew was said to purify the dead as they entered Hades. First-century poet Statius writes that the seer Amphiaraus, struck by Zeus's thunderbolt, died so quickly that the Fury who lived in a Yew grove had not had time to meet and purify him with a branch of Yew.

> *When the seer suddenly fell among pallid shadows,*
> *Invading the house of the dead . . .*
> *all were seized with horror.*
> *. . . for his limbs had neither*
> *Been consumed by fire nor came blackened from*
> *The sad urn, but were warm with the sweat of battle,*
> *His shield wet with blood and dust of the split plain.*
> *The Fury had not yet greeted and purified him with*
> *A branch of yew, nor had Proserpina* marked him*
> *By the dark gate as one of the company of the dead.*
> *His arrival even surprised the Fates at their spinning,*
> *And only on seeing the augur did the startled Parcae†*
> *Snap the thread.*

> PUBLIUS PAPINIUS STATIUS,
> *THEBAID*, BOOK VIII

---

*Proserpina is the Roman equivalent of Greek Persephone.
†Parcae is another name for the Fates.

Visions of Comfrey

I had an interesting experience while wrapping up my work on this section of the book—I was given a vision by a spirit who is working with me. It showed me that the herb Comfrey (*Symphytum officinale*), which is nicknamed "Knit Bone" and is a great bone and skin healer, can be scattered on the grave of a person who has died a painful death. The herb will bring solace and a release from pain. The living can use it too, externally in salves and poultices to heal sprains, broken bones, skin lesions, and wounds. Homeopathically prepared Comfrey is used to heal eye injuries. The raw herb contains pyrrolizidine alkaloids, however, making it unsafe for long-term internal use.

PART TWO

⁊

HERBS, FOODS,
AND TRADITIONS
OF SAMHAIN

RITUAL FOODS
FOR SAMHAIN OFFERINGS

Before we talk about foods for the Samhain feast, lets discuss a very important act of hospitality that should not be neglected—the sharing of food with your fairy neighbors and helpers. After all, Samhain marks the official end of the harvest and the labor of many, both seen and unseen, has gone into the successful fruition of the crops and produce.

According to tradition, the fairies "move house" at the fire festivals of Samhain, Imbolc, Beltaine, and Lughnasad, and they need a nourishing offering of food to sustain them at those times. A bowl of milk with honey (or a wee dram of whiskey), some oatmeal porridge with butter, or a selection of foods from your holiday feast are always correct. But any time you have a feast and especially on a holy day like Samhain, it is polite and correct to leave out a "spirit plate" for the fairies—a sampling of all the dishes you and your company are about to enjoy.

An offering of food for the fairies is best left at a fairy altar. Everyone needs to have a fairy altar somewhere in the house and also one in the garden or on a porch. If you have no porch or garden, then set your offerings beneath a large potted houseplant or under a tree in a local park. The food and drink may not always visibly disappear. Spirits live in a different dimension from us humans, and they may only partake of the essence of the food. On no account should a human eat the offerings once they have been set out for the Good Neighbors.

A Story of Mischievous Fairies

My longtime friend, who is known in certain nefarious circles as "Tipi Dan," sent me the following report of an encounter he had with one of the Good Neighbors.

True story: I was living in a tipi in winter outside Reno, Nevada, sitting in front of one of those little woodstoves, oval cylinders of sheet metal with a round regulator at the bottom and flippy lid on top. Sticks were piled up against the stove and the surrounding rocks that supported it. A pot of soup heating prevented me from opening the top lid: the regulator plug was off so I could feed sticks to the fire, and so I could watch the fire.

My soup began to boil so I gingerly moved the little enameled pot to the edge of the stove.

I sat to warm. My gaze drifted slowly to the open regulator. The tipi was dark, with the fire bright of flames and coals contained within a circle. My eyes roamed absently, coming to rest upon the woodpile. The pile of buff sticks was interesting—complex.

I stared at it emptily.

There, on top of the woodpile, sat a little brown man in a long-pointed cap with a long-pointed beard. Attenuated and thin, he kicked back, legs bent sharply at the knees in easy balance, arms to the side in the pose of an archaic dancer, as if to mock.

I reached to touch him, grasp him . . .

He disappeared before my eyes in an instant by turning into a stick on top of the woodpile, but he was able to spill my soup before he did.

This happened in 1984.

There are many kinds of fairies, of course—those who live in water, the spirits of air, and so forth. For the purpose of giving thanks for the harvest, it is appropriate to focus on land spirits—the Elementals who grow the plants, and the Danish and Norwegian Nisse, the Brownie or Broonie (Scots), the Swedish Tomte, the English Dobby or Hob, the

Irish Grogoch, the ones who work the land and help on the farm, and other unseen beings who move in and out and through the soil that nourishes all life.

Here are a few suggestions for offerings to these spirits at the festival of Samhain.

Apple
(*Malus* spp.)

Bury an Apple at Samhain as food for those spirits waiting to be born. See page 16 for more on the lore, history, and usage of Apple.

Grains and Potatoes

Leave the last of the grain and potato crop in the field as a gift for the fairies. After Samhain, the fairies leave a blight on all fruits left in the fields. It is forbidden to eat unharvested foods after Samhain, as the crops now belong to the sidhe. This is an excellent goad to make sure that everyone gets the harvest in!

Seaweed

It is particularly important for those who harvest or consume Seaweed to give thanks for this harvest from the sea. Fall (and spring) are traditionally the times of storms that throw up extra Seaweed onto the shore.

Offer a cup of ale or a bowl of porridge to Seonaidh (Anglicised to Shony or Shoney), celebrated as the god of the sea in the western isles of Scotland, in thanks for Seaweed and the health it brings. This is an especially powerful act when done in a storm. The offering is traditionally given at night.

In Scotland, Witches gather to do ritual on the "black shore," the liminal area between the line of seaweed on the beach and the sea.

There are many different ways to enjoy Seaweeds. I like to dry Kelp in the oven until it is crisp and eat it like potato chips. Try this with Dulse (*Palmaria palmata*) too. Both are rich in blood-building trace minerals. Carrageen (*Chondrus crispus*), sometimes called Irish Moss, is a traditional demulcent used for coughs, sore throat, and peptic ulcers. It can also be used as a substitute for gelatin to make elegant desserts.

To harvest and dry Carrageen: Look for it at low tide in summer. Cut it above the root, leaving enough of the stem so that the plant can continue to grow. Wash and rinse thoroughly, then place outside in the sun on a large piece of cloth (consider covering it with a single layer of cheesecloth to keep off flies) for 7 to 14 days. Sprinkle with water daily. As the Carrageen cures, it will go through many color changes. When everything is cream colored with just a few pink edges, take it indoors to dry in a sunny window or very slow oven for a few hours. Cut off any tough stalks and store the dried Carrageen in capped jars.

> **CAUTION: Many seaweeds (with the exception of Agar) have a lot of salt, and people with heart conditions should eat them sparingly, if at all.**

Here is an old Irish recipe that's low fat and gluten free.

🌿 Carrageen Lemon and Orange Pudding*

This recipe makes 4 servings.

> 1 cup dried carrageen
> ½ cup warm water
> 3 cups organic milk
> Zest and juice of 1 large organic orange
> Zest and juice of 1 organic lemon
> 3 tablespoons granulated organic sugar

Add warm water to the carrageen and allow it to soak for 15 minutes in a small bowl. As the seaweed is soaking, put the milk into a pan and bring it slowly to a simmer, stirring frequently so the bottom of the pan doesn't scorch. Set aside a teaspoon of the orange zest to use as a garnish.

---

*Adapted from Irish Dessert Lady's "Orange and Lemon Carrageen Pudding," Real Irish Desserts (website).

Add the soaked carrageen to the milk, along with the rest of the orange and lemon zests, stirring frequently. As the milk and carrageen mixture starts to thicken, add the sugar and lemon and orange juices. Keep cooking and stirring for about the next 20 to 25 minutes. Never allow the milk to boil, as that will destroy the carrageen's jelling properties.

After cooking for 20 to 25 minutes, strain the milk mixture into a jug or large bowl, discarding the used carrageen and cooked zest. Pour the pudding mixture into dessert bowls and allow them to set at least overnight before serving. (If you are using a mold, oil it lightly and pour in the strained mixture, allowing it to set for at least 24 hours.)

Garnish with the remaining orange zest.

🍃 Green Laver Soup*

Green laver (Ulva lactuca), sometimes called sea lettuce, is another seaweed that is often washed up on shore or harvested from tide pools. Once made into a pulp it is used to thicken soups. Why not make the soup in celebration of Shony, the sea god, after trekking to the beach to make an offering of ale and porridge to the waves? Serves 4.

To Make Green Laver Pulp

Gather several large handfuls of green laver and set them in a large pot or basin. Cover with water. Let soak for about 2 hours. Drain and rinse several times to remove any trace of sand.

Place the laver in a pot with water to cover by a few inches. Bring to a boil, then reduce the heat and let simmer, covered, for 2 hours. Add water as needed to prevent sticking and burning.

Drain the laver, transfer to a bowl, and mash with a potato masher or a large wooden spoon. Let it cool, then put it into a clean, capped jar. Store the pulp in the refrigerator, where it will keep for up to 10 days.

To Make the Soup

> 3¼ cups soup stock of your choice
> 1 cup green laver pulp
> 6 cloves organic garlic, peeled and mashed
> Sea salt and freshly ground white pepper

---

*Adapted from Pamela Michael, *A Country Harvest* (New York: Exeter Books, 1987), 132, 224.

Combine all the ingredients in a pot. Bring to a boil, then reduce the heat and let simmer, covered, for 45 minutes. Rub through a food sieve or food mill. Serve hot with crusty, whole-grain bread.

🍃 Agar (Kanten) Gelatin Dessert

This is a vegan dessert that I used to make in my old tipi days, when I went to Bard College. The advantage to the agar was that I could keep the dry flakes without refrigeration. I added wild blackberries, daylily blossoms, grated carrots, lemon, and honey. Agar (Gelidium amansii, among other species) is a seaweed sold in powdered or flaked form in supermarkets as a type of vegetable gelatin. Note: Agar powder is three times as strong as agar flakes. So, if a recipe calls for powder and you have flakes, you need to use three times as much. Serves 2–3.

> Vegetable oil spray, to prevent sticking
> 2 cups mixed berries, cut-up fruits, and grated raw carrot
> 1½ teaspoons agar flakes or ½ teaspoon agar powder
> 1 cup fruit juice or lemon-water-honey mix
> 1 cup water
> ½ cup organic sugar or ¼ cup raw, local honey

Lightly spray a bowl or mold with vegetable oil. Fill the bowl or mold with the fruit and grated raw carrot.

Combine the agar flakes, fruit juice, water, and sugar or honey in a pot. Bring to the boil, stirring constantly. Allow to boil for 2 minutes. Then pour the mixture over the fruit and carrots.

Transfer the bowl or mold to the refrigerator and allow the gelatin to set. Refrigeration is not strictly necessary as the agar will even set at room temperature. It should harden in just a few minutes. When it's ready, turn the bowl or mold upside down on a plate, and you will have an elegant and refreshing dessert.

Acorns

See the Oak profile beginning on page 47 for more on the lore, history, and usage of this tree and its Acorns.

Every year in late summer and early fall I gather Acorns to be made into cakes and breads. I have learned from experience that the best Acorns are still somewhat green; the brown Acorns are often already rotten inside.

I found several perfect stones at a local lake, the bottom one with a slight depression to hold the Acorn and a heavy top stone to smash the nut. I smash each nut separately, pick out the meat, and toss it into a bowl of water as I work (the water prevents the nutmeats from oxidizing). I listen to music as I do this; it takes many hours of labor. I collect the shells and later spread them on the garden.

I have often thought how pleasant this task would be if done with a whole clan or tribe. When I did this with my herbal students, we joked, laughed, and told stories all afternoon. That's what it must have been like for our ancestors for whom Acorns and Hazelnuts were their main source of carbohydrates.

When I finish smashing the nuts, I strain out the water and put the wet nutmeats into the blender with a bit of fresh, cold water. I blend the nuts into a coarse gruel. I fill glass jars halfway with the gruel and top them off with fresh water. I place the jars in the refrigerator for 2 weeks, straining the Acorn bits and changing the water every day.

When the Acorns have finished leaching, I strain the gruel thoroughly and spread it onto a large baking sheet, which I place in a slow oven (about 250°F) to roast and stir at intervals, until everything is completely dry, which takes 1 or 2 hours.

I store the dry Acorn meal in glass jars in the refrigerator until I want to bake, at which time I grind the meal in a coffee grinder to make a fine, powdery brown flour. The Acorn meal lasts about 2 years under refrigeration.

If you do not have access to Oak trees, Korean cuisine uses Acorn flour, so you may be able to purchase it from a Korean grocery store or online. You can decorate your Samhain altar with whole Acorns or make an Acorn cake and offer some to the ancestors and visiting spirits. Here is my favorite recipe, from my book *Secret Medicines from Your Garden.*

Plates 49 (left) and 50 (right).
Rowan Tree, Mountain Ash
(*Sorbus aucuparia*)

Plate 51. Rue
(*Ruta graveolens*)

Plate 52. Rutabaga
(*Brassica napus napobrassica*)

Plate 53. Sage
(*Salvia officinalis*)

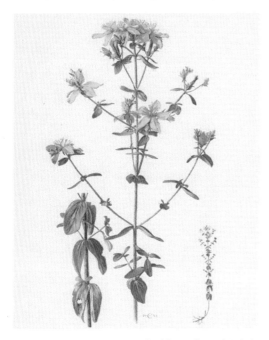

Plates 54 (left) and 55 (right).
Saint John's Wort (*Hypericum perforatum*)

Plates 56 (left) and 57 (right).
Star Anise, Chinese Star Anise
(*Illicium verum*)

Plate 58. Tansy
(*Tanacetum vulgare*)

Plate 59 (left). Thyme
(*Thymus vulgaris*)

Plate 60 (right). Tobacco
(*Nicotiana* spp.)

Plate 61. Turnip
(*Brassica rapa rapifera*)

Plate 62 (left). Vervain
(*Verbena hastata, V. officinalis*)

Plates 63 (top right) and 64 (bottom).
Violet (*Viola odorata*)

Plates 65 (left) and 66 (right).
White Cedar
(*Thuja occidentalis*)

Plate 67. Willow Tree
(*Salix* spp.)

Plate 68 (left). Woody Nightshade
(*Solanum dulcamara*)

Plate 69 (right). Wormwood
(*Artemisia absinthium*)

Plate 70. Yarrow
(*Achillea millefolium*)

Plate 71 (left). Yarrow
(*Achillea millefolium*)

Plate 72 (right). Yellow Dock
(*Rumex crispus*)

Plate 73. Yew
(*Taxus baccata, T. brevifolia,
T. canadensis*)

🍂 Acorn Cake*

1 cup acorn flour

1 cup other organic flour

1 teaspoon nonaluminum baking powder

1 teaspoon baking soda

½ teaspoon sea salt

½ teaspoon ground cardamom

½ teaspoon ground cinnamon

¼ teaspoon ground allspice

¼ teaspoon ground nutmeg

6 free-range, organic eggs

1 cup olive or coconut oil

1 cup raw, local honey

½ cup applesauce

1 cup organic sugar

Organic confectioners' sugar, to dust on top

Organic butter, to grease the pan

Grease and flour a Bundt pan. Preheat the oven to 350°F.

Combine the flours, baking powder, baking soda, salt, and spices in a bowl.

Beat the eggs, oil, honey, applesauce, and sugar together in a separate bowl.

Combine the wet and dry mixtures and mix well. Pour the batter into the Bundt pan. Bake for 30 to 40 minutes, or until a knife inserted in the center comes out clean.

Let the cake cool for 15 minutes and then turn it out of the pan onto a rack. Once the cake is completely cooled, dust lightly with confectioners' sugar.

Serve with maple walnut ice cream, vanilla ice cream, or freshly whipped cream as a decadent seasonal treat.

---

*Adapted from Danielle Prohom Olson, "Let Us Eat Acorn Cake! A Lazy Cook's Guide," Gather Victoria (website), November 4, 2014.

Hazelnuts

Hazelnuts are also appropriate for the Samhain altar and feast. Hazelnuts symbolize the "compact wisdom of the Druid": the inner nuts symbolize the Druid's brain, and the shell the Druid's skull.

There is an old Irish tale of a magical well under the sea that is surrounded by Hazel trees. The Salmon of Wisdom who live within the well eat the nuts as they fall in, and for every nut the Salmon eat, they develop another spot on their skin. This tale, like the story of the Well of Segais (also known as Connla's Well or the Well of Wisdom), may be references to a lost set of initiations undertaken by Druids as they gained secret knowledge.

It is said that ancient Druids carried Acorns and Hazelnuts on their person. I like to keep them in my coat pockets, and the cats also appreciate them as toys.

🌿 Hazelnuts and Brown Rice*

Serves 4.

4 tablespoons hazelnuts

1 cup organic brown rice

1–2 tablespoons organic butter

¼ pound organic mushrooms, sliced

A pinch of finely chopped garlic

1 tablespoon chopped organic parsley

Preheat the oven to 350°F.

Spread the nuts on a baking sheet and toast until they are fragrant and their skins are beginning to blister, 5 to 7 minutes. Let cool to room temperature, then use a cloth to remove the skins. Chop the nuts coarsely.

Cook the brown rice.

While the rice is cooking, heat the butter in a skillet over medium heat. Add the mushrooms and garlic and sauté until tender, 5 to 7 minutes.

When the rice is done, stir in the chopped nuts and sautéed mushrooms. Sprinkle the parsley on top before serving.

---

*Adapted from Pamela Michael, *A Country Harvest* (New York: Exeter Books, 1987), 64.

🍂 Hazelnut Cookies*

This recipe makes about 40 cookies.

> ½ cup hazelnuts
> ¾ cup plus 2 tablespoons organic flour
> A pinch of sea salt
> ½ cup (1 stick) cold unsalted organic butter, cut into small pieces.
> ¼ cup plus 3 tablespoons organic sugar
> A dash of vanilla extract or ground vanilla bean (optional)

Preheat the oven to 350°F.

Spread the nuts on a baking sheet and toast until they are fragrant and their skins are beginning to blister, 5 to 7 minutes. Let cool to room temperature, then use a cloth to rub off the loose skins. Chop and grind the nuts in a food processor or coffee grinder.

Combine the ground nuts with ¾ cup flour and a pinch of salt. Cut in the butter using two knives, and mix until the dough makes a ball. Divide the ball in half.

Combine the remaining 2 tablespoons flour with ¼ cup sugar and mix well. Dust a large work surface with half of the flour mixture. Roll out one half of the dough to make a log 11 inches long and 1 inch wide. Repeat with the rest of the flour mixture and the other half of the dough. Wrap the two logs in plastic and chill for at least 1 hour and up to overnight (or freeze for later baking).

Preheat the oven to 350°F.

Cut the logs into ½-inch slices and place on two baking sheets. Bake for 12 to 15 minutes, until the edges are slightly golden.

While the cookies are baking, pour the remaining 3 tablespoons sugar into a small bowl. When the cookies are done, let them cool for a few minutes, then dip each cookie into the sugar and set on a rack to finish cooling. Store the cookies in a tin; they'll keep for up to several weeks.

---

*Adapted from Maggie Ruggiero and Trudie Schwartz, "Hazelnut Cookies," Epicurious (website), May 2004.

The Dumb Supper
History, Modern Paganism, and Traditional Recipes

The version of the Dumb Supper that we'll talk about here is a distinctly modern Pagan idea. Christian Day writes about the history in *The Witches' Book of the Dead*.

> I found many references to the Dumb Supper throughout the twentieth century, but few had anything to do with the dead. The story generally involved a group of girls making a dinner of cornmeal and salt and eating it in silence, waiting for the "spirit" of their future husband to appear. If a girl saw nobody, she would never marry. If she saw "a black figure, without recognizable features," it meant that she "would die within the year." Other versions required every step of the meal to be set backwards. None involved the dead. . . .
>
> I was able to find only one story prior to the Wiccan revival of the latter twentieth century that involved a woman using the Dumb Supper to call up the spirits of the dead, and it was an African American folktale referenced in 1929. Prior to that point, one 1920 version alleged that supernatural signs might manifest, such as "two men carrying a corpse" or a "large white dog." . . .
>
> I later found British references to the "Dumb Cake," a ritual similar to the earliest references to the Dumb Supper, in that girls who

could stay silent while eating it would dream of their future husbands that night. In one instance, actual visages of future husbands supposedly would chase after the girls, while those who were to die unmarried would have terrible dreams of newly made graves.[1]

On the Isle of Man, the Dumb Cake was part of the Celtic New Year's celebration, called Hop-tu-Naa, that takes place on October 31. Folklorist Cyril Ingram Paton, who published a book on Manx traditions and history in 1942, tells us that the cake, called *soddag valloo,* was made and eaten in silence by young women. After eating it, the women silently walked backward to their beds, expecting to see their future husband in a dream or vision that night.[2]

A Dictionary of English Folklore has this to say about the custom of the Dumb Cake:

> One of the specialist forms of love divination, named after its central elements—the making of a special cake while maintaining absolute silence. Precise details vary, but the overall pattern is remarkably similar across the country and over the two or three hundred years since its first recorded mention in the 1680s. . . . Earlier recipes for the cake itself are generally more testing to the participants' resolve, including, apart from the salt, soot and even urine. Some mention the measuring of the ingredients in thimbles or egg-shells, presumably to make the cakes easier to eat.[3]

Perhaps simple indigestion led to light sleep, bad dreams, and visions?

The Dumb Supper in Modern Paganism

Traditional celebrations from the Celtic areas of Britain and Ireland to Poland, Mexico, and many other places honor the return of the dead to visit the living at Samhain. At this time, deceased loved ones, relatives, and neighbors may reappear in places that were once familiar to them: their old home, a favorite haunt, the cemetery where they are buried, or their familiar place of worship.

On Samhain it is considered polite and respectful to clean the house and hearth in preparation for a ghostly visit. Chimneys are swept clean, and doors and windows are left slightly ajar to provide easy entrance. Candles are placed in windows or set outside in lines that lead to the front door to guide the dead home, and a feast is prepared in their honor.

While these preparations are being undertaken, homeless beggars, unexpected guests, and guisers in fantastic costumes may show up at the door. These visitors must be shown all hospitality, because one never knows if they are the wandering dead, or even the gods in disguise. Food, drinks, and other small gifts should be provided to keep them contented and well fed.[4]

Modern Witches and Pagans have adopted the ritual of the Dumb Supper (that is, a silent dinner), an evening meal to honor the recently departed and beloved dead. At least one chair is left empty at the dining table for the exclusive use of the wandering spirits. Electric household lights are turned off, and only candles are used for illumination. Place settings may be deliberately turned around, such as putting the fork on the right and the knife and spoon on the left side of the plate, and dessert may be served first, followed by the rest of the courses in reverse order.[5]

In Celtic tradition, the number nine signifies death and transformation, and so a Dumb Supper should feature nine kinds of food on the table or foods made with nine ingredients. Below, you'll find some dishes to consider for the feast. A number of the recipes involve potatoes, a seasonal root vegetable appropriate for an "Underworld of the Fairies and the Dead" themed feast.

Traditional Recipes for the Dumb Supper

🍃 Colcannon*

Serves 4.

> 4 large organic potatoes, peeled and cut into chunks
> Sea salt
> 6 tablespoons organic butter, plus extra for serving

_____

*Adapted from Elise Bauer, "Colcannon," Simply Recipes (website).

3 cups chopped organic cabbage, chard, or kale

½ cup minced organic green onions (scallions)

1 cup organic milk, half-and-half, or cream

Put the potatoes in a large pot and add enough water to cover them by a couple of inches. Add a pinch of salt. Boil the potatoes until tender enough to pierce with a fork, then drain.

In a separate pot, melt the butter over medium-high heat. Add the chopped greens and sauté until they are wilted. Fold in the green onions and cook for 1 minute more.

Mash the potatoes with the milk. Mix the mashed potatoes into the greens. Season to taste with salt. Serve hot, with a large lump of butter in the middle of the dish. To eat, take a forkful of potatoes and greens and dip it into the butter.

🍂 Boxty Bread*

This traditional Irish potato bread should be served hot with plenty of butter. You will need some cheesecloth to drain the potatoes. The Irish word for "boxty" is bacstaí, and the name for the bread likely originates from the Irish arán bocht tí, meaning "poor house bread."

Makes 4 small loaves.

1¾ pounds organic potatoes

⅔ cup organic milk

2 teaspoons sea salt

½ teaspoon freshly ground organic black pepper

1½ teaspoons organic caraway seed (optional)

2 tablespoons organic butter, plus extra for serving

2¾ cups all-purpose organic flour, plus a bit more for
    kneading the dough

5 teaspoons nonaluminum baking powder

Preheat the oven to 375°F. Line a baking sheet with parchment paper.

Peel the potatoes; you could leave the skins on some of them for a slightly heartier bread. Set aside ¾ pound. Cut the rest into chunks and place in a saucepan. Cover with water, bring to a boil, and cook until they are easily pierced with a fork.

---

*Adapted from Mark Ebersole, "Irish Potato (Boxty) Bread," Mark's Daily Nosh (website), March 23, 2017.

While the potatoes are cooking, pour the milk into large bowl and add the sea salt, pepper, and caraway, if using. Mix well.

When the potatoes are done, drain them. Mash the potatoes with 2 tablespoons butter.

Grate the reserved ¾ pound potatoes into a piece of doubled cheesecloth and wring to squeeze out excess water. Stir the grated potatoes into the milk.

In a separate bowl, use a sifter or whisk to combine the 2¾ cups flour and the baking powder.

Add the mashed potatoes to the milk mixture and stir well. Add the flour mixture and stir until you have a smooth dough; the mixture should be slightly firm and pull together into a ball. If not, gradually add flour, bit by bit, until the dough has the right consistency.

Knead the dough lightly, then divide into four equal pieces. Roll each piece into a ball and then flatten each ball into a 4-inch circle. Place the circles on a prepared baking sheet. Cut a large X into the top of each loaf, about ½ inch deep.

Bake for 40 minutes or until golden brown. Serve warm, with plenty of butter.

🍂 Soul Cakes*

These sweet cakes are a favorite offering for the living and the dead at Samhain. They arise from the ancient tradition of "souling," when peasants and children would make the rounds in town, stopping at homes to beg for a "soul cake" and in return promising to pray for the souls of the household's departed. Souling is thought to have been the precursor or model for modern-day trick-or-treating.

> 1 cup (2 sticks) organic butter, softened (but not melted)
> 3½ cups sifted organic flour
> 1 cup organic sugar
> 1 teaspoon ground allspice
> 1 teaspoon ground cinnamon
> ½ teaspoon ground nutmeg
> ½ teaspoon saffron

---

*Adpted from Patti Wigington, "How to Make a Soul Cake for Samhain," ThoughtCo. (website), March 21, 2018.

2 free-range, organic eggs

3 tablespoons currants or raisins

2 teaspoons organic malt vinegar

Organic confectioners' sugar, for sprinkling on top

Preheat the oven to 350°F. Grease a baking sheet.

Cut the butter into the flour, using two knives. Mix in the sugar, allspice, cinnamon, nutmeg, and saffron. Lightly beat the eggs and add them to the flour mixture. Fold in the currants or raisins. Add the malt vinegar and mix until you have a stiff dough. Knead for a while, then roll out the dough to ¼-inch thickness.

Use a floured glass to cut out 3-inch circles of dough. Place on the greased baking sheet. Bake for 25 minutes. Remove from the oven and sprinkle with confectioners' sugar while the cakes are still warm.

🌿 Dumb Cake*

In 1892, the Reverend M. C. F. Morris, vicar of Newton-on-Ouse in Yorkshire, published his Yorkshire Folk-Talk, *in which he said of Dumb Cakes, "In the first place four people had to assist in the making of it, each taking an equal share in the work, adding small portions of its component parts, stirring the pot, and so forth. During the whole time of its manufacture and consumption a strict silence has to be observed. Even when it is being taken out of the oven each of the interested parties must assist in the work. When made it is placed on the table in the middle of the room, and the four persons stand at the four corners of the room. When set on the table the cake is divided into equal portions and put upon four plates or vessels. The spirit of the future husband of one of the four would then appear and taste from the plate of his future bride, being only visible to her whose husband he was destined to be. As a preliminary to this, every door of the house had to be thrown open. The traditional hour for making the feast was midnight."*[6]

Makes 1 9" layer cake.

5¼ cups organic all-purpose flour, plus extra for dusting
    the pans

4 teaspoons nonaluminum baking powder

---

*Adapted from Mattie Lee Wehrley, *Handy Household Hints and Recipes* (Louisville, Ky.: Breckel Press, 1916), 11.

½ teaspoon ground organic mace

½ pound organic butter, softened (but not melted)

3 cups organic sugar

2 cups organic whole milk

10 free-range, organic eggs

1 cup brandy

Icing of your choice

English walnuts and autumn leaves, for topping

Preheat the oven to 350°F for at least 20 minutes. Butter or oil two cake pans, then dust lightly with flour and shake off any residue.

Sift the flour, baking powder, and mace into a large bowl (or combine them in a bowl and whisk together if you don't have a sifter).

Cream the butter and sugar in a separate bowl. Add the milk, eggs, and brandy and mix well.

Add the flour mixture to the butter mixture. Mix well.

Divide the batter between the two prepared pans. Bake for about 40 minutes, until a knife or toothpick inserted into the center comes out clean. Rotate the cakes about halfway through the baking time to ensure even cooking.

When the cakes are done, remove them from the oven, invert, and cool on a baking rack. When the cakes are completely cooled, layer them with icing (I suggest a classic buttercream) and chopped English walnuts. Ice the top and sides. Garnish the top and the lower edge with English walnuts and autumn leaves.

🍂 Stwmp Naw Rhyw (Mash of Nine Sorts)

This Welsh dish calls for mashed potato, carrots, turnips, peas, parsnips, leeks, pepper, sea salt, and milk, half-and-half, or cream. Just boil up all the roots and mash them, except for the leek, which you sauté in butter and fold into the mash. Add in your liquid of choice for the desired amount of creaminess. For better flavor I suggest cooking each vegetable separately, which is more work, then mash everything together lightly. Think of it as a personal sacrifice on a high holy day.

The resulting mash is arranged in a circle on a large plate, and a ring is hidden inside the food. Unmarried party goers scoop up portions, and the one who gets the ring will be married within the year.

🍂 Vegetable Pancakes

These are simple pancakes made with a base of flour, milk, baking powder, sea salt, and grated cheese, with the addition of sautéed vegetables and herbs such as organic zucchini, onions, basil, and marjoram, served with sour cream on the side. The magical part of this dish is the nine ingredients.

🍂 Fruit Crepes

Any basic crepes will do. Fill them with mixed fruits, especially apples.

🍂 Horn-Shaped Baked Goods

The horned god is the god of the wild things and lord of the hunt. He is sometimes pictured as a stag with great antlers or as a man wearing antlers. He is the divine aspect of the animals who die so that we may eat and the grain and corn that once lived in the field before they were cut down for the harvest, which officially ends at Samhain. To honor the horned god, bake and offer cookies, cakes, breads, and other baked goods formed in the shape of a horn.

🍂 Bannock Bread (Oatmeal Bannock)*

Bannock is a large, flat, heavy fry bread from Scotland usually made from oats or barley. In one tradition, a bannock is baked, and one small section of it is charred in a flame. Then the bannock is broken up into pieces and the pieces are placed in a jar or a bag. Each celebrant reaches into the jar or bag to pick a piece, and the one who draws the burned piece must do the bidding of the company for the evening. Makes a loaf about the size of a large dinner plate.

> 1 cup finely ground organic oats
> ¼ cup organic, all-purpose flour
> ¼ teaspoon sea salt
> ½ cup organic buttermilk
> 1 teaspoon baking soda (no more than 6 months old, so
>   the bread rises more efficiently)

---

*Adapted from "Oatmeal Bannock (Scones Part 1)," *Baking for Britain* (blog), June 9, 2006.

Preheat your griddle. It is hot enough to cook on when flour sprinkled on it takes just a few seconds to brown.

Combine the oats, flour, and salt in a large bowl and mix well.

Put the buttermilk into a small bowl, add the teaspoon of baking soda, and mix briskly. Add the buttermilk mixture to the dry ingredients and bring together into a soft dough. Be careful not to overwork the mixture. Work quickly, as the baking soda will be kicked into action by the buttermilk.

Roll out the mixture on a lightly floured surface to a thickness of about ½ inch. Trim into a round shape (you can cut around a suitable-size plate).

Dust the griddle with a small amount of flour and put on the round of dough to cook. Cook on both sides until they brown.

🍂 Barmbrack*

Barmbrack is a kind of sweet raisin bread often associated with Halloween in Ireland. Small tokens may be hidden inside it. Since the walls between the worlds are thin at Samhain, it is a good time for divination, so small tokens are hidden inside the bread. A ring means marriage, a coin wealth, a small shred of cloth or a bean poverty, a pea means you will not marry this year, a matchstick means an unhappy marriage, a thimble means you will never marry . . . See if you can come up with your own symbolic tokens! (Be sure the objects you hide in your barmbrack are very clean, and warn your guests beforehand so they don't accidentally swallow them. This is probably not a good dish to serve to small children who could accidentally choke on something.)

Note that this recipe has nine ingredients!

2½ cups chopped dried, mixed fruit

1½ cups hot brewed black tea

2½ cups organic flour, plus extra for dusting the pan

1 teaspoon ground organic cinnamon

½ teaspoon ground organic nutmeg

½ teaspoon baking soda

1 free range, organic egg

¾ cup raw, local honey

1 teaspoon grated organic orange or lemon zest

---

*Adapted from Brooke Elizabeth, "Irish Barmbrack," AllRecipes.com.

Soak the dried fruit in the hot tea for 2 hours, then drain and gently squeeze out any excess tea.

Preheat the oven to 350°F. Spray a 9-inch Bundt pan with cooking spray and then lightly dust with flour for easy extraction.

Stir together the flour, cinnamon, nutmeg, and baking soda in a large bowl.

Beat the egg in a large bowl, then stir in the honey, citrus zest, and tea-soaked fruit. Gently fold in the flour until just combined. Pour the batter into the prepared Bundt pan.

Bake for 1 hour, until the top of the cake springs back when lightly pressed. Allow to cool in the pan for 2 hours and then remove the cake from the pan and let cool to room temperature on a wire rack.

If you're going to insert any objects into the barmbrack, clean them well and carefully press them into the cake through the bottom before serving.

Here is an American adaptation of the barmbrack for a Halloween party from 1905.

The Halloween Box Cake: The newest fashion in Hallowe'en supper-table decoration is a cake made of white pasteboard boxes, in shape like pieces of pie, which fit together and give the appearance of a large cake. Each one of the boxes is covered with a white paper which resembles frosting. At the close of the feast the pieces are distributed, each box containing some little souvenir suitable to Hallowe'en. One box, of course, contains a ring, another a thimble, a third a piece of silver, a fourth a mitten, a fifth a fool's cap, and so on. Much fun is created as the boxes are opened, and the person who secures the ring is heartily congratulated. The unlucky individual who gets the fool's cap must wear it for the evening.[7]

How to Conduct a Dumb Supper Ritual

So, you want to have your own Dumb Supper for your Coven, your Druid Grove, or simply for your friends and family. Here are some suggestions for how to conduct one. Please feel free to invent your own traditions!

The first step is to decorate the table. Nice touches would be skulls, images of skeletons and ghosts, black candles, black plates, black napkins, and a black tablecloth, if you have them. Fall flowers like Chrysanthemums are appropriate for the decor, as are Pumpkins, Squashes, Apples, Acorns, Hazelnuts, root vegetables of all kinds, and colorful fall leaves.

As you are planning the layout of the table, mark one chair to be left empty, as a seat for the honored dead who may visit. Lay out a place setting for the empty seat, but allow no one to use it.

Now you need to plan the menu. I have given a number of suggestions in the preceding chapter, but you could also think about seasonally appropriate fare like loaves of grainy brown bread, pumpkin and squash soups, root vegetables, and fall meats like venison or turkey.

Mulled cider, dark red wines, Apple cider, and mead are appropriate drinks for the fall table.

It goes without saying that cell phones and electronic devices should be turned off and left in another room, to eliminate distractions.

Electric lights should be shut off too; only candle flame, oil lamp, or hearth fire should be used for illumination.

Children should be invited to attend only if they can keep silent for the duration of the feast.

Start the ritual by going outside and making an offering to the local land spirits in thanks for their labors in bringing your harvest to fruition (see my suggestions in appendix A for suitable offerings).

Walk back to the house in total silence. The dining room should be treated as a ritual area by smudging it and the guests with Juniper, Sage, or other purifying herbs.

Call in the sacred directions (East, South, West, and North) or invoke the Celtic Three Worlds of Sacred Land, Sea, and Sky to establish your ritual space.* Call in the ancestors you wish to invite. Keep a door or window cracked open so the spirits can come and go at will. Do the invocations silently, for example the host or lead officiant can turn and face the directions, one at a time, while holding a wand, a large crystal, or a black feather.

At the place setting you have left for the empty seat at your table, each participant should light a candle in a jar in honor of their own deceased, silently offer up a prayer, and then leave a folded paper message for their beloved dead next to the candle. These messages can be burned in a fire later, sending them to the Sky realm via the smoke.

During the meal, which is eaten in complete silence, everyone should pay close attention to any messages, signs, or portents as they ritually share the supper with their living and deceased friends and family.

This ritual meal is a heavy responsibility for the host, who may wish to enlist a helper or two. The host should serve all the food as well as clear away the dishes, anticipating everyone's needs so as to preserve complete silence. No one should need to ask for something to drink or for an extra condiment like butter, salad dressing, or pepper and salt. These should be placed at intervals along the table, to be within easy reach.

---

*The Sacred Land is the realm of the animals, humans, plants, and nature spirits. The realm of Sea is the home of the fairies and the ancestors. The Sky realm is the home of the gods.

The spirits are served first, with a selection of every food on the table placed on a special "spirit plate" just for them (the spirit plate is put outside after the meal so the wandering dead may partake of the essence of the food). Then the oldest participants are served, and last the youngsters. No one should eat until everyone has a full plate and cup.

The host should silently clear away each plate and cup as the guests have had their fill.

The candles at the place of honor are allowed to burn themselves out, without interference.

After everyone has eaten, the guests should silently follow the host outside, where a ritual fire should be ready to be lit, or to a hearth indoors, and only the host should speak. This is the time to ask ritual questions such as, "If your ancestors could speak to you, what would they be saying now?" "In your life, what is dying away and leaving you?" and "What will you be dreaming of over the winter? And what practical steps will you take to manifest your dream?"

The guests should depart in silence, after perhaps taking a moment to write down the messages they have received (the host could have small pads of paper and pens laid out around the fire).

When everyone is gone, the host should thank the sacred directions or the Three Worlds, as well as the ancestors, and ritually sweep the house and fumigate with cleansing herbs like Sage or Juniper. While this is going on, a window or door must be cracked open to help speed the spirits back to their Otherworldly abode.

ᴀ Sample Samhain Rite

This is a Samhain ritual that I composed for the Order of White Oak (Ord na Darach Gile) in 1999.

Samhain Observance

The Samhain festival begins with offerings to the land spirits, for it is to them that we owe the bounty of the harvest, and after the feast all produce left in the fields shall belong only to the land spirits. Choice offerings of fruits, vegetables, and flowers shall be left on or near a stone or at an outdoor shrine in loving thanks for their labors.

Then shall the ancestor altar, which shall be maintained in the west of the house, be cleaned and decorated with photographs and mementos of the beloved dead, and all fires in the home shall be extinguished.

The high ceremony begins with the lighting of a mighty new fire. This fire shall be lit by women, in memory of Tlachta of Munster, daughter of Mogh Ruith the Druid, and nourished with oils, bees wax, dried herbs, or *uisce beatha** to feed its spirit. (In the event that the celebrants must remain indoors, the hearth or a cauldron may be used in which nine candles are placed and burned. Dried herbs may be fed to such a fire.)

---

*Uisce beatha is whiskey (literally, "waters of life").

The celebrants shall approach the fire in silence and then circumambulate it three times, stopping each time they reach the western point to recite the names of the beloved dead they wish to honor.

Then shall each celebrant place a small piece of paper or a suitable votive into the fire symbolizing their personal sacrifice for the new year. This sacrifice shall be an offering of service to the gods, the Earth, and her people.

Then shall each celebrant place a small piece of paper or a votive into the fire, sending their prayer skyward to the realm of the gods, signifying their personal petition for aid in matters of health, wealth, and affection, and one person shall remain with the fire until it is extinguished.

The celebrants shall then repair to a liminal space in the landscape: the top of a hill or mountain (between Earth and sky), by the black shore of the sea (between the line of seaweed and the water), by the shore of a lake, pond, stream, or river, in a cave, or in a field (between the house and the forest). There shall they cast divinations for the coming year. Those who of necessity must remain indoors may travel to a liminal space using a guided meditation.

Then shall a horned, masked figure appear out of the dark to lead the celebrants in a dance, and better it be that each celebrant dance in memory of an ancestor.

The celebrants shall then return to the house, where a meal is prepared. At this time the household fires may be relit using a brand from the ritual flames.

A place shall be saved at the table for the use of the beloved dead, and offerings of food and drink shall be set there. It shall be forbidden for any mortal to touch or consume this food.

A window or door must be left cracked open so that the spirits may easily enter and leave at their will. A candle placed in the window or by the door will guide the spirits to the house.

Traditional foods shall be eaten, especially foods with nine ingredients, for nine is the number of death and transformation. Small tokens may be hidden in these foods as a type of divination.

All honor must be shown to those who appear in strange and fantastic disguises, for they represent the wandering dead. These shall be entertained with food, especially Apples, symbolic of the Otherworld feast of Eamhain Abhlach.* And these Apples shall be offered floating in a vessel of sacred water.†

---

*Eamhain Abhlach (Emhain of the Apples) is an island paradise in Irish mythology, the home of Manannán Mac Lir, god of the headlands and son of the sea, who carries the dead across the waves to the Land of Youth.

†In this case, "sacred water" is water that has been ritually blessed, "sky water" collected during a rainstorm, or "wild water" from a stream, lake, river, or other waterway that has been boiled to sterilize it.

The Goddess at Samhain

For those who are more inclined to worship deities, the Celtic goddess most associated with Samhain is the Mórrigan (from Old Irish *mór,* "great," and *rígan,* "queen"). She is a triple deity, which in Indo-European thinking always means a high goddess (or god). Her three aspects are Badb Catha (battle raven), Macha (from the Old Irish *mag,* "plain"), and Némain (from the Old Irish *nemed,* "sacred"), sometimes translated as "frenzy." She is also a sovereignty goddess (a goddess who, representing a territory, confers sovereignty upon a king by marrying him or having relations with him).

As the Mare of Sovereignty, Macha was symbolic of sacred kingship. No Celtic king was legitimate until he had ritually married the land. In ancient times, a white mare was slaughtered after the new king had ritual sex with her. He then bathed in a broth made of her flesh and ate of it, thus becoming one with the sacred land. The fate of the king was always tied to the land; if the land suffered, the king could be deposed.

The Mórrigan is also associated with crows and ravens. After a battle the crows and ravens descend, looking to peck out the eyes of the dead and have their feast. The heads of slain warriors scattered about the battlefield were known as "Macha's mast" ("mast" as in scattered nuts on the ground that are food for pigs).

She is supremely powerful, prophetic, and magical. She will appear before a battle as the *bean-nighe* (washer at the ford) in the guise of a beautiful woman dressed in red, perched at the river ford, washing the armor and weapons of those about to die. She may also appear washing the cushions and harness of a battle chariot. When she lowers her hand, the river turns red as blood, and when she raises her hand, the river rises.[1]

As an all-powerful, magical deity, she takes on many guises, shapeshifting at will. Here is a description of Badb Catha from "Dá Choca's Hostel," an old Irish story of the kingship of Ulaid. In the story the king-to-be, Cormac Cond Longas, encounters the Badb in the form of an old woman washing a bloody chariot at the ford: ". . . a big-mouthed black swift sooty woman, lame and squinting with her left eye. She wore a threadbare dingy cloak. Dark as the back of a stag-beetle was every joint of her, from the top of her head to the ground. Her filleted grey hair fell back over her shoulder."[2] Shortly after this encounter Cormac spends the night at Da Choca's Hostel and is attacked and killed there.

Following is yet another description from a Scottish Gaelic ballad in which the Mórrigan appears in the form of a hag.

> *There were two slender spears of battle*
> *upon either side of the hag;*
> *her face blue-black, the lustre of coal*
> *and her lone tufted tooth was like rusted bone.*
>
> *In her head was one deep pool-like eye*
> *swifter than a star in a winter sky;*
> *upon her head gnarled brushwood*
> *like the clawed old wood of aspen root!*[3]

In the *Táin Bó Cúailnge* (*Cattle Raid of Cooley*), an old Irish epic, the Mórrigan approaches the god/hero Cú Chulainn as a beautiful maiden, offering to help him in the midst of a battle. When Cú Chulainn refuses her assistance, she swears to attack him in the future as an eel, a wolf, and a heifer, which she later does. She appears to him one day as a red-eared white cow (white animals, especially with red ears, are always a symbol of the Otherworld) with a retinue of fifty heifers. Then she attacks him in the shape of a huge, slippery black eel, and then as a gray-red wolf bitch.

Cú Chulainn succeeds in blinding her in both eyes, after which she appears to him in the guise of an ugly old woman milking a cow with three teats. Cú Chulainn asks for milk from each of the teats and blesses the old woman for her kindness, unwittingly healing her in the process. The Mórrigan then turns into a crow, sitting on a bramble bush.

Despite her efforts to destroy Cú Chulainn for rejecting her advances, at the time of his death, when he binds himself to a stone so as to remain upright in front of his enemies, she appears again in the form of a raven, perched on his shoulder. She stays with him until he expires, then flies away.

According to tradition, she met up with the Daghda at Samhain while she was washing in the river Unius of Connaght. She had one foot on one side of the river and the other foot on the opposite bank. There were nine tresses upon her head (we have already seen the significance of the number nine). They conversed and had sex, after which she advised him on how to defeat the Fomorians and offered her help in the battle.

A Ritual to Invoke the Mórrigan

This rite can be done at any time, but at Samhain it would be especially powerful. Other appropriate times would be at the full moon, at the dark of the moon, at dusk, or at midnight.

The Mórrigan is a death goddess who exults in the frenzy of battle. Death is a part of life that we must all ultimately face, and we cannot have rebirth without it. Like the Hindu god Shiva who dances as he destroys the universes, opening the way for Vishnu to dream in and Brahma to create new worlds, the death goddess opens the way for us so a new existence can emerge.

The Mórrigan is associated with crows, ravens, eels, cows, wolves, rivers, water, warriors, battles, prophecy, and weapons. Horses, sex, death, rebirth, shape-shifting, and sovereignty are also within her purview. Beautiful young women, powerful old hags, soldiers, physical fighters, those who fight for causes, and anyone who dies in a battle are in her sphere.

The Altar

Samhain is the beginning of the dark half of the year, and the Mórrigan is associated with black creatures: crows, ravens, and eels. Her sacred colors are red (for blood and the blood-red gown she appears in when she washes the weapons of warriors about to die) and black. Set up your altar with red or black cloth, red or black candles, black feathers, and a black bowl or cauldron filled with living water— that is, water from a well, river, lake, or stream. (If you can do the ritual outdoors, try scrying directly into a river, lake, or stream.) Place stones from a river bottom, streambed, or lake bottom at the base of the bowl or cauldron.

It would be a good idea to drink a strong cup of Mugwort tea before the rite to open your third eye/astral vision, and to purify yourself and the ritual space with Sage or Juniper smoke before and after the rite.

Start by grounding and centering. Pay attention to your breath for a few moments and soften your knees so your weight sinks, with your feet firmly planted on the ground.

Call in the four sacred directions (East, South, West, and North) or the Three Worlds (Sacred Land, Sea, and Sky) to establish sacred space. Those on a Celtic path will want to invoke Manannán Mac Lir to open the veil so the Mórrigan may more easily come through.

Depending upon your need and the focus of your rite, choose any of the sacred herbs of Samhain listed in this book. You may simply wish to communicate with the goddess, or you may be looking for protection from something, or seeking to honor a deceased relative, and so on. Place the herbs in a dish and send the smoke to her, wafting it with a black feather.

As you silently or verbally communicate with her, imagine yourself shape-shifting into a crow or raven. Feel the feathers growing from your arms as you fly to her and tell her of your need.

Soften your vision so that you see not only in front of you but also on the periphery as you gaze into the bowl of water. Look at the surface of the water. Pay attention to your feelings, emotions, thoughts, what you see, and any messages you might hear.

Hear the goddess asking you, "What will you give to me for these gifts I have given you?"

Think about what you will do differently in your life and in the world, in her honor.

When you have received your answer, give thanks to the goddess and to Manannán Mac Lir, asking him to close the veil so that only good spirits can remain. Then thank the Three Worlds or the sacred four directions. Leave a gift of nourishment for the goddess and for the spirits of place upon the altar.

When the rite is done, pour the water upon the Earth, and keep the stones for future workings.

APPENDIX A

OFFERINGS FOR THE LAND AND WATER SPIRITS

Offerings for the Land Spirits

The land spirits feed us and heal us and nurture our homes and gardens with their beauty. In return, we make offerings to the sacred land in every season, not just at Samhain. Any time your home faces danger, an important event is anticipated, or a journey planned, offerings of thanks and protection should be given. Whenever your family or tribe has a feast or performs a ritual, offerings should be made. Leave a plate of food or place offerings on the Earth so the nature spirits, fairies, house elves, and other kinds of good helpers feel honored and included.

Any of the gifts described in "Ritual Herbs for Samhain Offerings" would be appropriate to offer on an altar. In addition, you can leave offerings, prayers, and messages with the trees. Hang *cloots,* or rags imbued with hopes and prayers, in the branches of a sacred tree, or hang stones with natural holes in them or other talismanic items for varied purposes. Different trees have different properties and relate to distinct times of the year, and indeed, the offerings can be altered as the year progresses and the hopes and thoughts come to fruition, or not.

We all have an ever-changing relationship with Nature and our personal environment. If you live in an area where the land and the local spirits have been abused or neglected, you can hang cloots or other objects with healing messages for the spirits of the place.

Here are a number of simple offerings you can make to the spirits of place.

- When going on a hunt or fishing, make an offering of part of the catch as the Earth too must be fed.
- When planting a tree, give it a gift of Rosemary and Thyme if you can. But any herbs will do if offered with reverence and care.
- Bury butter and other offerings at the boundary of your land as you ask for blessings and protection from the land spirits.
- Offer mead or whiskey. If it's mead, make sure it's made from local honey; the land spirits understand local. Offer a bit of good bread with the liquor. Or mix up some good local milk with a little honey and a shot of whiskey added to it.
- On Turtle Island (America), the land spirits recognize Tobacco, so offer it freely.

Offerings to Sacred Water

In Celtic regions, sacred wells and springs are often decorated with white stones (quartz) and flowers on the holy days. There is a saying that "all white stones belong to the fairies." Other appropriate offerings to holy wells include pine cones, coins, keys, buttons, beads, pipes, fish hooks, jewelry, religious objects, fruits, and flowers. Offerings of cheese, barley cakes, or other foods may be left for the spirits of sacred waters after a ritual.

Offerings to Rivers

Every river—indeed, every natural waterway—is under the protective care of a particular goddess. To express gratitude to your local river goddess, you might offer flowers, fruits, silver, and other natural or local items.

For more information about offerings for the various land and water spirits, see my book *Scottish Herbs and Fairy Lore* (Los Angeles, Calif.: Pendraig Publishing, 2010).

APPENDIX B

OFFERINGS FOR THE FAIRIES AT EACH SABBAT

Samhain, Lá Samhna, Calan Gaeof
(October 31)*

Make offerings to a sacred fire of dried herbs, whiskey, and butter or ghee.

Make offerings of Rosemary (for memories) to the fire.

Leave a dish of the feast for the ancestors.

Pour red wine, honey, cider, or milk in the fields and on stones.

Offer ale and oatmeal gruel to the sea in thanks for the Seaweed and the fish.

Leave a little of the harvest in each field and in the water.

Leave a blessing for the trees.

Make an offering to the fire of a bunch of dried herbs and wild plants that have hung on a wall in your home for the previous year. In August and September of each year, gather new ones from your herb garden and the roadside, dry them, tie them together, and hang the new bunch on the wall for the next year.

---

*Or November 11 in the old style.

Winter Solstice, Yule,
Meán Geimhreadh, Alban Arthan
(December 21)

Make offerings to and sing to trees, especially Apples.

Hang fruits and birdseed on the trees for the forest spirits.

Make offerings of Mint or Cinnamon to the fire.

Pour wine, honey, cider, or milk in the fields and on stones.

Recite poetry for the trees.

Participate in lots of shouting and noise to wake up the spirits and drive away blight.

Later, on Twelfth Night, which is January 5 (or more traditionally January 17, the old date from before the introduction of the Gregorian calendar in 1752), hang toast in the branches of Apple trees and pour cider over their roots to give them a drink.

Imbolc, Oimelc,
Lá Fhéile Bride, Calan Gaeaf
(February 1–2)

Make offerings to a sacred fire of dried herbs, whiskey, and butter or ghee.

Pour milk offerings on stones.

Make offerings of incense to the fire.

Place a basket by the hearth or door filled with shortbread cookies, dried fruit, and Brighid's crosses to delight Brighid as she passes by.

Pour port wine, honey, cider, or milk in the fields.

Wake the Earth with your staff by pounding the ground three times.

Sing or recite poetry to the trees.

Offer a Corn Dolly made at Lughnasad to the Earth at Imbolc, burying it in the soil after saying a few words. Corn Dollies are made from stalks of wheat with the grain still on them. When buried, they grow the wheat for the following Lughnasad. (Of course, if you live in a more northern latitude you should wait for the appropriate season to plant your Corn Dolly. In New England they say you can safely do this when "Oak leaves are the size of a mouse's ear.")

Spring Equinox, Meán Earrach, Alban Eilir (March 21)

Make offerings to a sacred fire of dried herbs, whiskey, and butter or ghee.
Offer ale and oatmeal gruel to the sea.
Pour milk offerings on stones.
Pour wine, honey, cider, or milk on the gardens and fields.
Bless seeds and plant them in unexpected places.
Draw your wishes on fertile eggs and bury them in the ground.

Beltaine, May Day, Lá Bealtaine, Calen Mai (May 1)*

Make offerings to a sacred fire of dried herbs, whiskey, and butter or ghee.
Offer butter or milk to rocks.
Make offerings of Apple blossoms, Rose flowers, or anything in bloom to stones, trees, gardens, and fields.
Pour mead in the fields and on the stones.
Make and offer incense to the fire.
Make offerings of flowers and fruits to water and wells.
Leave a blessing for the trees.
Offer May wine, milk, and honey for the land spirits.

---

*Or May 12 in the old style.

Summer Solstice, Litha, Midsummer, Meán Samhradh, Alban Hefin (June 21)

Make offerings to a sacred fire of dried herbs, whiskey, and butter or ghee.

Pour milk offerings on stones.

Pour white wine, honey, cider, or milk on the gardens and fields.

Children can welcome the nature spirits at the time of the summer solstice. They may play music and circle-dance around an Apple tree decorated with crystals as a way to show gratitude, wear their finest fairy garb, and light candles to float in a big tub of water as a beacon to welcome the local spirits.

Lughnasad, Lammas, Lunasa, Lá Lúnasa, Calen Awst (End of July to Second Week of August)

Make offerings to a sacred fire of dried herbs, whiskey, and butter or ghee.

Pour milk offerings on stones.

Climb a high mountain and leave offerings of quartz, flowers, fruits, and grain.

Offer butter to lakes.

Offer flowers, fruits, and coins to water.

Float a wreath down a river.

Float a small wooden boat with candles and flowers down a river.

Decorate standing stones with wreaths or garlands of wheat.

Offer a loaf of the new grain.

Make offerings of the first harvest, such as vegetables and herbs.

Pour stout, honey, cider, or milk in the fields and on the stones.

Make Corn Dollies; feast on breads, cheese, and baked goods; and leave out a dish for the land spirits.

Leave blessings for the trees.

Fall Equinox, Meán Fomhair, Alban Elfed (September 21–22)

Make offerings to a sacred fire of dried herbs, whiskey, and butter or ghee.

Pour milk offerings on stones.

Offer ale and oatmeal gruel to the sea.

Pour ale, honey, cider, or milk on the gardens and fields.

Make a scarecrow from the new grain and place it in the exact center of your fields. Do not give it clothes. The spirit of the Grain will inhabit the scarecrow and look out for the welfare of the crops.

Gather fresh herbs and hang them on a wall; keep them there until Samhain of the next year, when they will be burned in the ritual fire.

Fall Equinox is the middle of the harvest; offer the first fruits, roots, and grains you gather. The "second harvest" is often hard fruit, such as Pears and Apples, and a lot of vegetables, especially root crops.

Have a harvest swap, bake bread, drink cider, and offer a portion of everything to the spirits.

NOTES

An Introduction to Samhain, the Otherworld, and the Power of Herbs

1. "Halloween Divination in Ireland," The Fading Year. *Irish Folklore: Calendar Customs, Traditions, and Beliefs* (blog), October 31, 2016.

Herbs for Protection from and Communication with the Sprits and Fairies

1. Paul Melvin Wise, "Cotton Mather's Wonders of the Invisible World: An Authoritative Edition" (dissertation, Georgia State University, 2005), from the ScholarWorks @ Georgia State University online archive (website).
2. Ovid, *The Metamorphoses of Ovid,* translated by Michael Simpson (Amherst: University of Massachusetts Press, 2001): book 7, page 118.
3. Eugene Zampieron and Ellen Kamhi, "Topical and Oral Herbal Pain Remedies," *International Journal of Alternative and Complimentary Medicine* 1, no. 4 (2015): 21.
4. Sarah Anne Lawless, "Six Herbs for Spirit Work," *Sarah Anne Lawless* (blog), November 11, 2015.
5. Donald Alexander Mackenzie, *Wonder Tales from Scottish Myth and Legend* (New York: Frederick A. Stokes Co., 1917), 184.
6. Tony Lock, "Folklore of the Hedgerow: Blackthorn," Folklore and Traditions of the Irish Hedgerow (website).
7. Sarah Anne Lawless, "Six Herbs for Spirit Work," *Sarah Anne Lawless* (blog), November 11, 2015.
8. "Protection of Houses against the Evil in the Region of Mazovia," *Lamus Dworski* (blog), November 18, 2017.
9. "Old Nance and the Buggane," Feegan's (website).
10. Benjamin Slade, trans., "Woden's Nine Herbs Charm" (from the

Lacnunga 79–82), as published on Herot.dk (website), August 27, 2002.

11. Thordur Sturluson, "Fumitory—Herbal Uses and Benefits," The Herbal Resource (website).

12. Linda Crampton, "English Ivy Symbolism, Traditions, and Mythology," Owlcation (website), March 13, 2017.

13. "What Is the Meaning of a Ghost Bead Necklace Created by the Navajos?" Reference.com (website).

14. Laurel Morales, "To Get Calcium, Navajos Burn Juniper Branches to Eat the Ash," *The Salt: What's On Your Plate* (blog), from NPR online, August 21, 2017.

15. "Lichen Mythology," Ethnolichenology, Fandom (website), July 7, 2013 (information cited from Nancy J. Turner, Randy Bouchard, and Dorothy I. D. Kennedy, *Ethnobotany of the Okanagan-Colville Indians of British Columbia and Washington,* Occasional Papers of the British Provincial Museum no. 21, Province of British Columbia, 1990).

16. Christopher Hobbs, *Usnea: The Herbal Antibiotic and Other Medicinal Lichens,* 3rd rev. ed. (booklet) (Capitola, Calif.: Botanica Press, 1990), online at Dr. Christopher Hobbs (website).

17. Paul Melvin Wise, "Cotton Mather's Wonders of the Invisible World: An Authoritative Edition" (dissertation, Georgia State University, 2005), from the ScholarWorks @ Georgia State University online archive.

18. Pliny the Elder, *The Natural History,* translated by John Bostock and H. T. Riley, Perseus Digital Library, book 16, chapter 95, "Historical Facts Connected with the Mistletoe."

19. Crystal Aneira, "Magickal Uses for Mullein," *Herbal Riot* (blog), May 28, 2015.

20. "Protection of Houses against the Evil in the Region of Mazovia," *Lamus Dworski* (blog), November 18, 2017.

21. Leimomi Oakes, "A Smock of Nettles," *The Dreamstress* (blog), April 4, 2014.

22. Melissa Snell, "How to Avoid the Plague: Two Dozen Tips That May or May Not Help," ThoughtCo. (website), updated May 2, 2018.

23. "The Origins of Halloween Part 1: Samhain and the Celtic Time of Spirits," The Ancient Web (website), October 31, 2010.

24. Ellen Evert Hopman, *Scottish Herbs and Fairy Lore* (Los Angeles, Calif.: Pendraig Publishing, 2010).

25. "The Bards of Ireland," *Dublin Penny Journal* 1, no. 3 (July 14, 1832).

26. Deidre Larkin, "The Medieval Garden Enclosed," *Metropolitan Museum of Art* blog, November 7, 2008.

27. "Celtic Mythology: Five Sacred Guardian Trees of Ireland," *Stair na hÉireann/History of Ireland: Irish History, Culture, Heritage, Language, Mythology* (blog).

Herbs of Purification

1. Mrs. M. Grieve, "Basil, Sweet," from *A Modern Herbal* (1931), as published on Botanical.com.
2. Justin Faerman, "Tulsi (Holy Basil): The Sacred Indian Superherb that Harmonizes Your Mind, Body and Spirit," Conscious Lifestyle Magazine (website).
3. "Krishna Tulsi—Health Benefits and Medicinal Uses of Fresh Tulsi Leaves," *Ayurvedic Upchar* (blog).
4. "Basil in Hoodoo, Voodoo, Wiccan & Pagan Rituals: Folklore and Spells," *Art of the Root* (blog), July 23, 2015.
5. "Rue," WebMd (website), accessed December 13, 2017.
6. Pliny the Elder, *The Natural History,* translated by John Bostock and H. T. Riley, Perseus Digital Library, book 20, chapter 51, "Rue: Eight-Four Remedies."
7. "Sage," Witchipedia: The Online Encyclopedia of Witchcraft, Paganism, and the Occult (website).
8. "Sage," WebMd (website).
9. "Sage," WebMd (website).
10. "Vervain," *Eldrum Tree* blog.
11. Pliny the Elder, *The Natural History,* Loeb Classical Library (website), book 25, chapter 59, 215–16.
12. "Verbena," WebMd (website).
13. Anne McIntyre, quoted in Ilana Sobo, "Yarrow: Ancient Herb of Healing, Protection, and Power," *The Alchemist's Kitchen* (blog).
14. "Yarrow," WebMd (website).

Visionary Herbs and Herbs of Divination

1. Chris Bennett, "The Scythians—High Plains Drifters," *Cannabis Culture Magazine* 2 (summer 1995), as published on the website of the Herb Museum (Vancouver, Canada).
2. "Mugwort," WebMd (website).
3. Desmond Boylan, "A Modern Witch," Reuters (website), August 19, 2013.
4. Anne Charlton, "Medicinal Uses of Tobacco in History," *Journal of the Royal Society of Medicine* 97, no. 6 (Jun 2004): 292–96.

Herbs to Communicate with, Release, and Honor the Dead

1. Crystal Aneira, "The Magical Uses of Belladonna," *Herbal Riot* (blog), June 23, 2013.

2. "Belladonna Folklore," Belladonnakillz.com.

3. John Brand, *Observations on Popular Antiquities: Chiefly Illustrating the Origin of Our Vulgar Customs, Ceremonies, and Superstitions,* vol. 3 (London: Charles Knight and Co., 1842), 8.

4. "Belladonna," WebMd (website).

5. "Belladonna," in online version of William Boericke's *Homeopathic Materia Medica,* 9th edition (1927), presented by Médi-T through Homéopathe International website, 1999.

6. Richard Folkard, *Plant Lore, Legends, and Lyrics: Embracing the Myths, Traditions, Superstitions, and Folk-Lore of the Plant Kingdom,* 2nd edition (London: Sampson Low, Marston & Company, 1892), 95. From the online PDF at the Electric Scotland website.

7. Aleister Crowley, *Magick without Tears* (a series of letters from Crowley written in the 1940s and published in book form in 1954, after his death), as reproduced on Biblioteca Pleyades (website).

8. Helena P. Blavatsky, *The Theosophial Glossary* (London: Theosophical Publishing Society, 1892), 93.

9. "Sacred Tree Profile: Hawthorn (Lore, Medicine, Magic, and Mystery)," *The Druid's Garden* (blog), October 30, 2015.

10. Mara Freeman, "Tree Lore: Hawthorn," Order of Bards, Ovates, and Druids (website).

11. "Hawthorn," WebMd (website).

12. Dean Ravenscroft, "Lotus Flower Meaning and Symbolisms," Lotus Flower Meaning (website).

13. April McDevitt, "Lotus," Ancient Egypt: The Mythology (website), last updated August 17, 2014.

14. Noted in "Papyrus Paintings from the Book of the Dead," Time Trips (website), from the Egyptian Book of the Dead, spell 81A: Spell for Being Transformed into a Lotus.

15. Noted in "Papyrus Paintings from the Book of the Dead," Time Trips (website), from the Egyptian Book of the Dead, spell 185: Giving Praise to Osiris.

16. "Lotus," WebMd (website).

17. Gabriel Mojay, *Aromatherapy for Healing the Spirit: Restoring Emotional*

and Mental Balance with Essential Oils (Rochester, Vt.: Healing Arts Press, 2000), 94.

18. Michele Meyers, *Oregano and Marjoram: An Herb Society of America Guide to the Genus* Origanum (Kirtland, Ohio: Herb Society of America, 2005), 10–12.

19. J. Hill, "Sobek," Ancient Egypt Online (website), 2010.

20. "Per-Sobek," Sesh Kemet Egyptian Scribe (website).

21. "Marjoram," WebMd (website.)

22. Crystal Aneira, "Magikal Uses of Althea," *Herbal Riot* (blog), September 30, 2013.

23. Richard Folkard, *Plant Lore, Legends, and Lyrics: Embracing the Myths, Traditions, Superstitions, and Folk-Lore of the Plant Kingdom,* 2nd edition (London: Sampson Low, Marston & Company, 1892), 434. From the online PDF at the Electric Scotland website.

24. Henry Cornelius Agrippa, *The Philosophy of Natural Magic,* edited by L. W. de Laurence (1913) from Sacred-Texts.com (website), chapter XLIII, 137.

25. M. Isidora Forrest, "Isis and the Magic of Myrrh," *Isiopolis: A Votive Work in Honor of the Goddess Isis* (blog), July 20, 2013.

26. Gary J. Lockhart, *A Woman's Herbal Guide* (1989), as edited and reproduced in a PDF online by Arthur Lee Jacobson (2007), 8. From the online PDF at Arthur Lee Jacobson (website).

27. Lynn R. LiDonnici, "Single-Stemmed Wormwood, Pinecones and Myrrh: Expense and Availability of Recipe Ingredients in the *Greek Magical Papyri,*" *Kernos* 14 (2001), 61–91.

28. "Myrrh," WebMd (website).

29. Sarah Chavez, "Parsley—The Herb of Death," *Nourishing Death* (blog), December 30, 2013.

30. "Parsley," WebMd (website).

31. "Pasque Flower," Eldrum Herbs (website).

32. "Pulsatilla," WebMd (website).

33. Thodur Sturluson, "Lesser Periwinkle—Medicinal Uses and Benefits," Herbal Resource (website).

34. Thodur Sturluson, "Lesser Periwinkle—Medicinal Uses and Benefits," Herbal Resource (website).

35. "The Pine Tree," Theosophy Trust Memorial Library (website).

36. Jessy Moore, Michael Yousef, and Evangelia Tsiani, "Anticancer Effects of Rosemary (*Rosmarinus officinalis* L.) Extract and Rosemary Extract Polyphenols," *Nutrients* 8, no. 11 (Nov. 2016): 731.

37. "Rosemary," WebMd (website).

38. "Star Anise," WebMd (website).

39. Roy Vickery, "Tansy," Plant-Lore: Collecting the Folklore and Uses of Plants (website), 2010.

40. Harold A. Roth, "Tanacetum vulgare, Tansy," Alchemy Works (website), accessed January 2, 2018.

41. "Tansy," WebMd (website).

42. "The Legend of Violet—The Flower," *A Piece of European Treasure*, an online textbook of the European interdisciplinary curricula.

43. Quoted in Markus Hartsmar, "Oscar Wilde, 1854–1900," Absinthe.SE (website).

44. "Wormwood," UsesofHerbs.com (website).

45. "Protection of Houses against the Evil in the Region of Mazovia," *Lamus Dworski* (blog), November 18, 2017.

The Dumb Supper:
History, Modern Paganism, and Traditional Recipes

1. Christian Day, *The Witches Book of the Dead* (San Francisco, Calif.: Red Wheel/Weiser, 2011).

2. Cyril Ingram Paton, *Manx Calendar Customs* (London: Folk-Lore Society, 1942; reprint by LLanerch Press, 2004).

3. Quoted in "Dumb Cake," Oxford Index (online).

4. "Dziady/Zaduszki/Pominki—The Forefathers' Eve," *Lamus Dworski* (blog), October 31, 2015.

5. "Samhain 'Dumb Supper,'" *Celtic History* (blog), October 31, 2014.

6. Rev. M. C. F. Morris, *Yorkshire Folk-Talk* (London: Henry Frowde, 1892), 230.

7. Sarah Chavez, "Halloween: Death Makes a Holiday," *Nourishing Death* (blog), October 20, 2013.

The Goddess at Samhain

1. Anne Ross, *Pagan Celtic Britain* (New York: Columbia University Press, 1967), 314.

2. Quoted in Anne Ross, *Pagan Celtic Britain* (New York: Columbia University Press, 1967), 317.

3. Quoted in Anne Ross, *Pagan Celtic Britain* (New York: Columbia University Press, 1967), 297.

OTHER BOOKS
AND RESOURCES
FROM ELLEN HOPMAN

For more on preparation methods, dosages, harvesting techniques, cautions, and many other helpful herbal details, please see the following books.

A Druid's Herbal for the Sacred Earth Year, by Ellen Evert Hopman (Rochester, Vt.: Destiny Books, 1995)

A Druid's Herbal of Sacred Tree Medicine, by Ellen Evert Hopman (Rochester, Vt.: Destiny Books, 2008)

Scottish Herbs and Fairy Lore, by Ellen Evert Hopman (Los Angeles, Calif.: Pendraig Publishing, 2010)

Secret Medicines from Your Garden: Plants for Healing, Spirituality, and Magic, by Ellen Evert Hopman (Rochester, Vt.: Healing Arts Press, 2016)

The Secret Medicines of Your Kitchen, by Ellen Evert Hopman (London: mPowr Ltd., 2012)

Tree Medicine Tree Magic, by Ellen Evert Hopman (Los Angeles, Calif.: Pendraig Publishing, 2017)

Walking the World in Wonder: A Children's Herbal, by Ellen Evert Hopman (Rochester, Vt.: Healing Arts Press, 2000)

For detailed information about Druids and Druid practice, please see:

A Legacy of Druids: Conversations with Druid Leaders from Britain, the USA and Canada, Past and Present, by Ellen Evert Hopman (Alresford, UK: Moon Books, 2016)

For an enjoyable peek into Iron Age spirituality, please see the following trilogy of Druidic novels with Iron Age herbal healing, prayers, rituals, and practices woven into each story.

Priestess of the Forest: A Druid Journey, by Ellen Evert Hopman (Woodbury, Minn.: Llewellyn Worldwide, 2008)
The Druid Isle, by Ellen Evert Hopman (Woodbury, Minn.: Llewellyn Worldwide, 2010)
Priestess of the Fire Temple: A Druid's Tale, by Ellen Evert Hopman (Woodbury, Minn.: Llewellyn Worldwide, 2012)

For details about ancient and modern witchcraft, please see:

Being a Pagan: Druids, Wiccans, and Witches Today, by Ellen Evert Hopman (Rochester, Vt.: Destiny Books, 2001)
The Real Witches of New England: History, Lore, and Modern Practice, by Ellen Evert Hopman (Rochester, Vt.: Destiny Books, 2018)

Ellen Evert Hopman's classes, books, workshops, bio,
and blog can be found at www.elleneverthopman.com.

For information on Druid instruction and initiation online
and in person, visit www.tribeoftheoak.com.

INDEX OF PLANTS
BY COMMON NAME

INDEX OF PLANTS
BY SCIENTIFIC NAME

Numbers in *italics* preceded by *pl.* indicate color insert plate numbers.

GENERAL INDEX